C000228484

The
Reluctant Farmer
of
Whimsey Hill

BRADFORD M. SMITH
with
LYNN RAVEN & NANCY RAVEN SMITH

"Animals can and do make our lives better. This is my kind of book."
– Bret Witter, co-author of #1 NYT Bestseller - *Dewey (the Library Cat)*

ALSO BY THE AUTHORS

BENCH TIPS FOR JEWELRY MAKING
by Bradford M. Smith

MAKING DESIGN STAMPS FOR JEWELRY
by Bradford M. Smith

LAND SHARKS - A SWINDLE IN SUMATRA
by Nancy Raven Smith

KP AUTHORS COOK THEIR BOOKS - Anthology
by Nancy Raven Smith

SUMMERCHASE (Available 2017)
by Lynn Raven

THE RELUCTANT FARMER
OF WHIMSEY HILL

THE RELUCTANT FARMER
OF WHIMSEY HILL

by

Bradford M. Smith

with

Lynn Raven and Nancy Raven Smith

Published by Whimsey Wylde
Santa Monica, California

Published by Whimsey Wylde
Santa Monica, California

Printed in the United States of America

Cover Artist: Jean Abernethy

Cover Design: LimelightBookCovers.com

For my loving family
with all our crazy animals and for all the people
who have made my journey through life happy,
interesting, and a true joy.

And a warm thanks to those
who assisted in making
"The Reluctant Farmer" possible.

TABLE OF CONTENTS

THE RELUCTANT FARMER
OF WHIMSEY HILL

Life begins at the end of your comfort zone.

- Neale Donald Walsch

PROLOGUE
HOW NOW BLACK COW

1971

If a black cow crosses your path, is it worse luck than a black cat?

I'm not a superstitious man. And yet, here I stand in the middle of the road about a mile away from our farm in rural Virginia wearing my best navy pinstriped suit.

Doesn't sound like such bad luck, does it?

But if this were a good news, bad news thing, that would actually be the good news. The bad news lies at the other end of the thick rope I'm clutching in my hands.

That's where it circles the neck of a Black Angus steer named Pork Chop.

There's no doubt in my mind that this unruly beast was put on earth to torment me.

My family disavows all connection to Pork Chop. They refer to him as "my cow," as in, "Honey, your cow is out" or "Daddy, your cow needs to be fed." Somehow this animal has managed to alienate my entire family. Not an easy feat with a family as besotted and overrun with animals as mine is.

But for once, Pork Chop is not being rowdy. Actually, quite the opposite. He's lying on his side with all four feet stuck out stiffly. He looks dead, but he's just asleep. I can see his chest rising and falling steadily. Dead might be easier to deal with.

Judging by the long shadows cast by the nearby pine trees, it'll be dark soon.

Pork Chop weighs nearly six hundred pounds, and there's no way I can move him on my own. As much as I'd like to, I can't leave him lying in the road to go for help. He could be injured or cause an accident. But if I don't go for help, who knows how long I'll be stuck here. Pork Chop isn't my family's favorite animal, yet they'll never speak to me again if he gets hurt.

A honk shatters the quiet. A neighbor slows down in his dusty, battered Ford pick-up.

I raise my hand to wave him down. He waves back and drives on. I can see him snickering in the rear view mirror.

Our working farm neighbors don't know what to make of me. I'm still the outsider who works nine to five for the federal government.

I can understand their confusion. The country is not my habitat of choice. As a Boston native and a Cornell graduate with a Masters in Electrical Engineering, order, logic, and cleanliness matter to me. The robots I work with suit me perfectly. When I program them, they do what they're supposed to. Robots never pee, poop, bite, kick, or drag me where I don't want to go.

Unfortunately my wife's animals do.

1

BRAD PLANS, GOD LAUGHS

Four Years Earlier

Normally, I don't attend "singles" dances. They're always uncomfortable with too much emphasis on making connections and too much pressure to score. But tonight, I let some co-workers cajole me into attending a Junior Officers and Professionals Club singles event at the old Roosevelt Hotel in Washington, D.C.

It's a decision I'm already regretting. This dance is the same as any other I've ever attended - pleasant, but boring. The ballroom is uninspiring and shows years of hard use. The ladies I've met tonight are nice but not memorable. I guess they could say the same about me. At twenty-five, with dark brown hair, medium height, average looks, and build, I must seem like just another guy to them. Another few dances and I'm out of here.

The DJ starts playing Frankie Valli's "Can't Take My Eyes Off Of You," a favorite of mine. I glance around for a new partner just as two blondes and a brunette enter the hotel ballroom. I'll learn later that one of the blondes is the first runner-up for the Miss Virginia crown. Yet it's the brunette who appeals to me.

I intercept her and ask for a dance. It's a split-second decision with unimagined consequences. Her name is Nancy and we fit together well. For me, the dance ends all too soon.

After the music stops, we politely thank each other and move on to meet other partners. Two more dances and I'll leave, I decide. Yet while my next partners in their Jackie O dresses are attractive, I find myself thinking about Nancy.

She seems a bit on the shy side, but while we were dancing, we both admitted we were dragged to the event by friends. And she laughed happily at one of my old jokes. That sky-rockets her right to the top of my list.

Not that I have a list. I'm not looking for a serious relationship. I've mapped my life out into increments. First college, currently a tour of duty in the Navy as a Lieutenant, Junior Grade, followed by what I hope will be a high-paying job in industry.

Besides, it's 1967. The Vietnam War rages on, and the Navy can ship me out at a moment's notice. People I know are questioning the validity of the war. I don't know what to think, but I'm ready to do my duty. A serious relationship will have to wait until my tour is over.

That said, there's no reason I can't enjoy the company of pretty women while I'm stationed in D.C.

After a few more dances, I find myself searching the room for Nancy instead of leaving as I had planned. I locate her dancing near the DJ. She's surprised when I cut in.

"Hi," I begin. Oh, I forgot how blue her eyes are.

She smiles. "Hi, Brad."

She remembers my name. That's a good sign.

"I'd like to see you again," I say.

Six simple little words.

2

YOU AIN'T NOTHIN' BUT A HOUND DOG

Within a month, Nancy and I are dating regularly. We're having a good time, but then I discover she owns a dog. If that isn't bad enough, I find she has a horse, too. This is not good.

Animals have never played a part in my life. A cat scratched me badly as a child, and I've had no interest in pets since. My Mother raised some dogs, but I rarely interacted with them. To be fair, the rockets and fireworks I used to make as a boy, along with the smells from my chemistry set, probably made them avoid me too.

While small animals and I mutually steer clear of each other, horses are a whole different matter.

When I was eleven, my father took me along on a visit to a farm owned by his friend, Farley. I noticed there were several horses on the farm and Farley asked if I'd like to ride. I thought of Gene Autry and Roy Rogers, my favorite TV cowboys.

Absolutely I wanted to ride like they did.

Seconds later, Farley tossed me up on a horse that seemed gigantic at the time. Everything looked different from the back of this tall, muscular animal. It was amazing.

Farley led the horse out of the barn and into an open field. The pleasure I was feeling ended abruptly when he turned the horse loose, slapping it on the rump. The horse didn't like that, and away we went at a full gallop. Well, let's just say he took off and I fell off.

My second encounter with a horse was even worse. I was a high school senior when a classmate suggested we go riding. I was older and stronger than when I had visited with Farley. I thought wouldn't have any trouble controlling a horse now, so I agreed.

The ride started out nicely. We crossed the paved road in front of the stable and walked out into a large meadow and then along a gas pipeline that had cleared space on both sides of it.

But later when we turned around to head back, things changed rapidly. My horse decided it was in a hurry. First its walk quickened, then he started to trot. I was getting bounced all over and nearly sliding off, so I pulled back on the reins to stop, but it wouldn't. My friend was behind me, and yelling for me to stop. Fat chance. The horse totally ignored the reins and my cries to whoa. Instead, he went faster and faster. Before long I was hanging on for dear life.

Suddenly I spotted the road in front the stable up ahead. I jerked the reins as hard as I could, but to no avail. My horse never paused. I closed my eyes and prayed there were no cars coming.

I heard a screech of brakes and the clatter of my horse's hooves on the pavement, but there was no impact. When I forced myself to open my eyes, I wished I hadn't. We were racing up the stable driveway.

I managed to hang on until the horse came to a sliding halt outside the closed barn door. I imagine there's still a dent in that door where I hit it.

An hour later, my knees were still shaking. That was the most terrifying few minutes I've ever experienced. There's no way I want anything to do with horses.

So a girlfriend with pets is not a plus in my book, but the fact fades into the background the first time we kiss. Unfortunately, as we date more, her animals do start intruding.

First there's Amy, her butterscotch-colored, medium-sized, rescue dog.

"What breed is she?" I ask politely the first time I pick up Nancy.

"A Golden Heinz."

"I hear they're nice dogs."

Three months later I learn Nancy's definition of a Golden Heinz. "Golden" stands for yellow and "Heinz," as in the old Heinz Ketchup ads, "We have 57 kinds," stands for mixed breed mutt. Hence, Amy is a yellow mutt. Nancy never said anything, but it's clear I blew it.

Golden Heinz or not, Amy hasn't exactly warmed up to me.

Whenever I'm at Nancy's apartment, Amy inserts herself between us, or stands a little off to the side, watching me closely. Have you ever tried to kiss a woman with a pair of disapproving eyes staring at you? Avoid it at all costs. It really throws you off your game.

When I confide my problem to a coworker, he suggests I call a veterinarian and ask for help. Not a bad idea, but I feel too embarrassed to do it.

Yet Amy's behavior finally bothers me so much that I do stop at a pet store for advice. After I carefully describe my problem to the freckled teenage clerk, she breaks into a fit of the giggles.

Catching my annoyance, she recovers her composure.

"How about a box of doggie treats? Food should make the dog like you."

Of course. Why didn't I think of that? It's perfectly logical.

"What do you recommend?"

"These are the most popular ones." She hands me a box of treats shaped like dog bones from the shelf.

"Perfect. How much?"

"Ten dollars plus tax."

Ten dollars for dog biscuits? What's in them, prime rib? I barely manage not to blurt that out loud.

I hesitate, but Nancy's face floats into my mind and I reach for my wallet.

I exit the pet store with as much dignity as I can muster. The sound of the Clerk giggling again follows me out.

**

"Treats for Amy? What a nice thought," Nancy gushes when I arrive at her place. I get one of those excellent kisses for my efforts. Mentally I pat myself on the back. Mission accomplished.

Amy, however, is still standoffish. She cautiously accepts a treat as if it might be laced with poison, then backs away to where she can watch me. As she slowly chews, her disapproving stare never wavers. Not once. No wagging of the tail or licking (God forbid) of the hand. Nothing. Definitely an ungrateful reception for a ten dollar box of treats.

I'm relieved Nancy doesn't seem to notice. But then she says, "Did you know animals are the best judges of character?"

She wouldn't dump me just because her dog doesn't like me - would she?

I decide to return to the pet store tomorrow for more advice, and ask for the manager this time. Nancy interrupts my thoughts.

"Are you free this weekend? Would you like to meet my horse, Junior?"

As compared to what? Matches under my fingernails, a root canal?

To my horror, "I'd love to," rolls out of my mouth.

At least I won't have to get on the horse and, if it doesn't like me, it won't matter. It lives in a barn far away. Out of sight, out of mind. Right?

3

WELCOME TO MY NIGHT MARE

The weekend starts simply enough considering I'm going to see a horse. Still, I might lose Nancy if I don't.

Copying the original advice from the giggly pet store clerk, I stop at the Safeway in McLean to buy carrots on my way to meet Nancy at the barn. Food is logical to me. It hasn't paid off yet with Amy, but hopefully it will with the horse. If Junior doesn't like my carrots, well, tough. As with Amy, my real goal is to impress Nancy.

I'm not even sure how one "meets" a horse. You can see a horse or touch a horse, but "meet" a horse?

Still, I'm learning how important Junior is to Nancy. She's an amateur equestrian who competes at the national level. In her case, that means she rides horses over very, very big jumps in horse shows up and down the Mid-Atlantic States. Her focus is on her horse and training for the next competition, not on her job as receptionist at the CBS News Bureau in Washington.

Since I'm intense about my own work at the Carderock Navy lab, designing software for manufacturing ships and planes, I can sort of understand her passion. So if it makes her happy, I'll visit the silly horse.

And I'm getting to know Nancy's best friend, Sharon, a little better. Sharon's tall and willowy, with sandy blond hair. She's truly nice and, like Nancy, she attended American University in the art program. Sharon's a fine artist and does beautiful oil paintings of animals.

One day Sharon warns me of an unusual quirk Nancy has. Apparently, Nancy frequently breaks dates to go riding. Her dates will arrive to pick her up only to find a note taped to her apartment door, "Sorry, gone riding." Sharon's surprised that I've lasted so long without receiving one.

If that's true, and Nancy ever has to choose between her horse and me, does that mean the horse would win? Not exactly a comforting or reassuring thought.

Still, there are those kisses. And she hasn't stood me up yet. I consider that a good sign.

In an effort to show Nancy I'm taking the 'meet the horse' occasion seriously, I carefully dress in nice clothes and even shine my shoes for the event. Thank goodness none of my friends can see me. I'd be laughed out of my lab, not to mention the Navy.

Nancy boards her horse, Junior, with the Tompkins family at their farm across from Madeira, a private girls' school, halfway between McLean and Great Falls, Virginia. She met the Tompkins when she taught riding to the students at Madeira.

I enjoy the drive to the Tompkins' place. After heavy overnight thunderstorms, today's spring weather is sunny and warm. The twenty-minute drive there on Old Georgetown Pike passes through woods filled with blooming dogwood trees, past sprouting fields, and out into the Virginia buffer area between suburbia and the truly rural countryside.

Arriving at the barn early, I park my older Volvo I bought from my parents when they upgraded and look around. Nancy's gray Volkswagen is parked by the fence. There are lots of horses munching grass out in the fields, but I don't see any people. I do hear hammering.

Following the sound leads me to a decrepit, putrid green horse van. It's sort of an ancient box on wheels with interior room for three horses. Its better days were decades ago.

The banging comes from inside. I get closer and look in. There's Nancy, on her knees, nailing a two-inch thick wooden plank down on the floor.

"What are you doing?" I ask.

She shrugs. "One of the boards broke."

"How'd you learn to do that?"

"I figured if I copied the way the other boards are laid, it wouldn't be a problem to fit one in, and then I strengthened the rest." Like it's no big deal. I admit I'm impressed. Here's a five-foot, four-inch tall, one-hundred-twenty pound woman swinging a hammer as comfortably as any guy I've ever met. This at a time when most young women have high bouffant hair with enough hairspray to hold their coiffures motionless in an open convertible at sixty miles an hour.

I grew up with a father and a grandfather who taught me to build and repair things, so it's second nature to me. But none of my dates ever owned a hammer, much less knew how to use one. This girl is definitely different. I can't decide if that's a plus or a minus.

I realize she's looking at me.

"Whose truck is this?" I ask as something to break the silence.

"Sharon's and mine."

Oh?

"It had a blown motor, so we paid a friend of a friend to repair it. Now it's ours."

"Who drives it for you?"

"I do."

Really? In the 1960s, a woman driving a large truck is very unusual, odd even.

When I mention this, she gives me a funny look.

"It's just like driving a car, only bigger." Maybe to her because she's used to driving a stick shift. Automatic shifts are the rage in the new cars, and most people don't bother to learn manual shifting anymore. And most young women I know wouldn't be caught dead at such a "masculine" activity as driving a truck.

"What kind of response do you get?" I ask.

"Mostly people smile and laugh at me. The only time I ever had trouble about it was when I took Junior to Madison Square Garden in New York. The motor had some problems, and I had to find a mechanic. After I unloaded Junior at the Garden and put her in her stall, I drove to a truck garage. When I got there, there were a dozen or so male truck drivers standing around. There was no smiling or laughing and a lot of hostile stares directed at me when they saw a woman behind the wheel. It was tense, but luckily nothing happened."

Lucky indeed, I think.

She lays down her hammer, and climbs down to give me a welcoming hug. The carrots receive a warm smile and a kiss, just as I had hoped.

Holding hands, we walk to a nearby paddock. The fenced area forms a "U" that wraps around the far end of the Tompkins' barn. Nancy whistles as we enter and closes the gate behind us.

I'm told this is barn rule number one. If you go through a gate, you always leave it in the same position. Closed gates are closed behind you, and open gates are left open, unless you know the situation and are knowingly changing it. Now that she explains it, I can relate. In my lab, I deal with computers telling machinery how to work. If anyone came in and changed the settings and switches, it could be a disaster.

Her bay mare, Junior, trots over to us.

I recognize Junior from the pictures on the wall in Nancy's apartment. Yet they didn't prepare me for the real thing. Nancy calls Junior a small horse at 15.2 hands, but Junior's head towers over me.

As Nancy feeds her, Junior's immense teeth easily crunch through the thick carrots.

Sharon's horse, Bear, ambles over for his share. Bear is a huge chestnut, even bigger than Junior. Nancy and Sharon pooled two hundred dollars to buy Junior while they were in college. It didn't faze them that show horses cost tens of thousands of dollars. They just kept looking until they found a horse they thought had potential. Later, they pooled their money again to buy Bear, and now each has a horse.

I already knew Junior's official show name was Double Conspiracy. The "Double" for Nancy and Sharon, and "Conspiracy" because neither Nancy's nor Sharon's parents knew they owned a horse while they were in school.

The nickname, "Junior," was shortened from "Nancy Junior."

That name came from Clarence, an older groom at Madeira School where Nancy taught riding on weekends and summers. Teasing Nancy, he claimed the mare was as stubborn and contrary as she was. So he always called the horse Nancy Junior and shortened it later to just Junior as it was easier to say than Double Conspiracy and it stuck.

When they bought her, Junior was an unbroken four-year-old, running wild on a Blue Ridge mountain top near Culpeper, Virginia. Now, Junior is a well-traveled, prize-winning show horse who has been in numerous competitions, including the Super Bowl for equines-Madison Square Garden in New York. Nancy tells me they aren't always big winners, but the mistakes are hers, not Junior's. Still, they win enough to make it fun.

I mumble what I hope are the appropriate compliments while nervously petting Junior and Bear. Nancy offers to let me feed the carrots to the horses. I force myself, but I have flashing visions of those huge teeth crunching through my hand. I'm relieved when the carrots are gone, and all my fingers are still attached.

Sensing the end of the treats, Junior and Bear wander out of sight around the far end of the barn. I sincerely hope the "meet the horse" part of the day is over.

Nancy and I stand talking beside a particularly large puddle left by last night's rain. Now that we're done with the horses, I can relax and enjoy the fresh, clear day.

I'm especially appreciating the twinkle in Nancy's eyes while she talks.

Suddenly her eyes widen. "Run!" she yells, dragging me backwards by the sleeve.

Behind me, I hear the thunder of pounding hooves. I turn. A half ton of horse gallops directly at me. I freeze. Nancy's hands continue tugging, but it's too late.

Her horse, Junior, hits the enormous mud puddle beside me with all the anticipatory delight of a mud wrestler. Once there, she pauses just long enough to bounce up and down in a frenzy, covering me in mud from head-to-toe.

Then Junior races away, disappearing again behind the far end of the barn.

Seconds later, she peeks from behind the corner.

Nancy yells again, "Run!" I don't have to be told twice. This time I dash for the fence and climb up.

Junior charges like a freight train straight for the puddle. Again, she hops up and down in it, gleefully spraying mud everywhere.

I'm outraged. "She did that deliberately."

Nancy's mortified. "I'm so sorry. I totally forgot how much Junior loves splashing people."

What? She knew this might happen and didn't say anything? Furious, I point out, "Horses can't love things."

"Junior has a weird sense of humor."

Now the horse has a sense of humor, too? Get real. I don't buy any of it and say so.

I earn a quick, disapproving look.

Irritated, but struggling to keep it inside, I try to maintain my composure while casually wiping a glob of thick mud out of my hair.

Nancy tries to suppress a smile.

It isn't funny. I scrape more mud from my clothes. My good shoes are totally ruined.

She smiles again, followed by an explosion of unbridled laughter. I crack a grin, and then a chortle. Okay, so maybe it is funny. Soon we're both laughing hysterically.

"You don't believe Junior splashes people deliberately? I dare you to go stand beside the puddle again." She challenges me.

17

I glance over at the puddle. Junior ambles in the distance to graze near Bear. It must have been an accident. I just overreacted.

"You'll notice that Junior isn't interested in the puddle unless there are people near it." I

Look again. She doesn't seem to be.

Nancy slides off the fence.

"Watch." She slips quietly toward the puddle. Not quietly enough. Behind her, I can see Junior's head come up immediately. Before Nancy's halfway there, Junior is in motion.

I don't think Nancy sees how quickly Junior responded. She pauses near the puddle and turns to wave at me.

"Run!" I yell.

That's when she spots Junior.

Nancy bolts for the fence, but Junior's faster. SPLAT! All four hooves hit the mud. SPLAT! SPLAT! As the mare leaps happily up and down.

Now Nancy's as drenched and filthy as I am.

I can't help myself. The sight of her sadly standing there covered in mud cracks me up. I laugh.

She gives me a rueful glance as she climbs back on the fence. I help wipe the slime from her face.

To her credit, she giggles. It's low at first and then erupts into laughter. That's one of the things I'm coming to like about her. She laughs easily and often, at herself as much as anything else. She has a clear sense of the ironic and the absurd.

She indicates Junior. "When I was first trying to ride her, Junior would buck me off once a day, every day, but only once. After I hit the ground, she would stand there waiting for me to pick myself up and remount. For the rest of the ride, she'd behave perfectly, but it was only a matter of time before I got seriously

18

injured.

Then Sharon noticed that right before Junior bucked, she'd flatten her lower lip. That was something I couldn't see from her back. So Sharon and I worked out a warning system. She'd sit on the fence while I rode, watching for Junior to flatten her lip. When she did, Sharon would yell, 'Bombs away!' and I would quickly jump off.

After three days of 'Bombs away!' Junior has never bucked again while ridden. If I wasn't going to play, it just wasn't fun for her anymore. Junior's not a normal horse. Junior is Junior."

I know I'm naïve about horses, but I'm not that gullible. In spite of watching Junior play in the mud puddle, I know horses are just big, dumb animals. Unfortunately, I make the huge mistake of saying so. Needless to say, the rest of the day does not go well.

Next week, I show up promptly for our dinner date. As I raise my fist to knock on Nancy's door, I see a note.

It reads, "Sorry. Gone riding."

4

POP GOES THE QUESTION

Not a quitter, I manage to survive the "Sorry. Gone riding" note with roses and an apology.

I even manage to bite my tongue and refrain from asking her if she ever left a note on Junior's stall door saying, "Sorry, gone dating." There might not be enough roses in the world for me to recover from that one.

In spite of all of my misgivings about Amy and Junior, Nancy and I totally enjoy each other's company. Clearly, she moves to the beat of a different drummer more than any other woman I've met. If I had to describe her in one word, that word would be "unconventional." She's not interested in the party invitations she gets. In fact, in the six months we've been dating, she's turned down most. Money doesn't impress her. She always looks great, but she's not into clothes or make-up.

Yes, I'm hooked. Probably because she's one of the few people I've ever met who's truly happy. She follows her passion. She doesn't look to others for approval, she just does her own thing.

I also discover that she's incredibly introverted and very uncomfortable around groups of people she doesn't know. Maybe that's what makes her avoid parties and relate so much to her animals. I'm not sure why she's comfortable with me, but I'm truly glad she is. Of course the fact that she thinks I'm handsome doesn't hurt my ego either.

Amy still refuses to be my friend, and Junior exists happily in her paddock without any repeat mud episodes involving me. They don't matter anymore.

I'm in love. So much for my long laid plans. I think we can live on a Lieutenant's salary if we're careful. I hope Nancy won't mind penny-pinching until I make the move to the private sector and can earn a better income. More worrisome is the possibility of a posting to Vietnam, but I wouldn't want to be reassigned and not tell her first how I feel. I'm going to propose.

I have it all planned out. Tonight I'm taking her to the Junkanoo Polynesian Restaurant for dinner. It's one of our favorite places in D.C. Then we'll dance at the Three Thieves Club and end the evening with a walk along the Tidal Basin near the Jefferson Memorial. That's when I'll ask her. I have a speech prepared, and I've been practicing all day. I have everything carefully planned.

The ring is safely tucked in my pocket. It's an emerald in what the salesman calls a Tiffany setting. I picked a green stone because Nancy prefers colored stones to diamonds, which she thinks are cold. I thought the color would remind her of the green fields where she likes to ride.

The evening arrives. I'm cool, calm, and ready. I knock on Nancy's door. Thank goodness there's no "Gone riding" note tonight.

Nancy opens the door and we hug. I don't want to let go. She feels and smells soooo good.

"You look especially nice tonight," she says.

"Will you marry me?" blurts out of my mouth.

Damn, I thought. How stupid is that? I totally blew it.

"Yes."

Did she say something?

"Yes?"

"Yes," she repeats.

The rest of the evening passes in a fog of euphoria. I have small mental snapshots like the sparkle of the ring on her finger, the twinkle in her eye, but most of the evening passes in a blur.

We feel like a pair of conspirators and can't stop grinning. We have a special secret that only the two of us know. Tomorrow will be the calls to our parents and friends. Tonight it's just us. It's a closeness that's as joyous as two kids at Christmas and we've received the ultimate gift: each other.

Toward the end of the evening, Nancy reminds me of a trip we'd taken to see my parents. I was headed up to see them in Erie, Pennsylvania, and I asked her along for the weekend. Make that Nancy and Amy. She doesn't go anywhere without the dog.

Interestingly, my mother and Amy became instant best friends. I'd forgotten how much she loves dogs. Weirdly, Nancy and my Mother also share a funny physical characteristic. Neither of them sits in the usual Indian style on the floor. I believe that's also called the Lotus position with your legs crossed in front of you. Instead, both of them sit with their legs bent straight out to the side with their knees flat on the floor. Kind of frog style.

My Dad noticed and commented on it. I was surprised because I'd never made the connection before when I saw Nancy sit like that.

On the way home, Nancy and I made a fun sightseeing detour to see Niagara Falls. Over all, it was a pleasant weekend. So why is she bringing it up now?

Nancy laughs. "You don't know how much our engagement owes to a fortune cookie."

Huh?

"It happened after we went to meet your parents."

"What do you mean? We had a great time up in Erie."

"We did, but I expected you to say something about moving our relationship to the next level afterwards. When you didn't say anything, I thought I'd failed the parent test."

"There's a parent test?"

"Usually when a guy takes his girlfriend to meet his parents, it means she's special. I was hurt when you didn't say anything. So I was going to break it off. I told Sharon my decision when we were eating lunch down in Chinatown. After lunch, two fortune cookies came with the check.

Mine read, "Be patient. His intentions are true." I took that as an omen and told Sharon I'd give you two more weeks. You made it by one day. She grins.

I'm more than a tad skeptical of the fortune cookie story. I'm even momentarily annoyed that she would make up such a silly tale. Remembering the trouble I was in when I expressed doubt about Junior's antics, I smile and let it go.

When we return to her place, she shows me the paper from the fortune cookie. I can't believe that's what it actually says.

"Be patient. His intentions are true."

5

GOODBYE CITY LIFE

The next day, we're confronted with questions from friends and family about our engagement. Questions to which we have no answers yet.

"When is the wedding?" Everyone asks, pretending not to be surprised.

"Big wedding or small wedding?" My mother, thinking of friends to invite.

"Church? Elope?" Her older, married sister.

"You're kidding, right?" Her older, married brother. Totally incredulous.

"Okay, now I believe in fortune cookies," Sharon.

"Married? You?" Followed by peals of laughter. My single co-workers.

"How many in the wedding party?" Her mother, already planning the wedding.

"Really?" Her disbelieving single friends.

"How much?" Her father, adding the wedding bills up in his head.

"Please, no purple tuxes." My father, thinking of his sister's wedding party.

And the most serious question of all.

"Where are we going to live?" Nancy and I.

We both have roommates, so our own places aren't an option.

One night, snuggled on my couch, we discuss the subject.

"How about renting a townhouse or an apartment?" I begin.

Mmmm. I like it when she blows in my ear.

"Only if it has a yard for Amy."

"That makes sense. We can do that." Ahh. Her kisses. They're nice too.

"Of course it would be smarter to move to a farm."

Not for me, it wouldn't. Luckily I don't say that out loud.

"If we did, we could save the money on Junior's board."

Not necessary. I consider that money well spent. I like Junior out at the Tompkins farm. Far, far away. Mmmm. Kiss me again...

"I wouldn't have to spend all that time and energy driving out to the barn every day."

True. I can think of other uses for her time and energy.

"I could sleep in later and be home for dinner earlier."

Yes, that might be nice.

Her hands rub my back.

The idea is sounding better. Mmmm. And better.

"You'll love living on a farm," she says.

Uh, oh. No. No farm. I'm a city boy. I like Chinese take-out and pizza delivery, the theater, wine tasting parties, my friends...

"No. I don't want to live on a farm." I get out before she gives me another long kiss.

"Give it a chance. You'll love it. Think of the money we'll save."

Saving money is good. Living anywhere near Junior? Not so good.

"No farm."

Her hand strokes my neck.

"How about a compromise?" She asks. "Let's rent one for a year. If at the end of the year, you don't like living in the country, we'll move back to the city. Deal?"

"One year...?"

"That's all," she whispers in my ear. "It'll be fun. You'll see."

Mmmm. What was that? What will be fun? I'm all for fun. "Okay. Yes,"

"Thanks, Honey. You won't regret it. You'll see."

Wait. I won't regret what? Oh, rats. Did I agree to a farm?

6

SPLISH, SPLASH

Nancy and I concentrate our search for a rental farm in the area around Great Falls, Virginia. It's about half an hour from my lab and about four miles further out into the country on Route 193 than Junior's current home at the Tompkins'.

Not too bad a drive. Of course, I'd prefer less of one, but I did promise to give it a year.

That's something that still mystifies me. How on earth did I ever agree to live on a farm? No matter how many times I think about that evening I agreed to a farm, it's still not clear to me why I said yes.

My friends razz me. What am I thinking, they want to know. They say they'll never see me again if I move to the country. I tell them it's only for a year. I'll be back so quick, they won't even miss me.

Secretly, I worry my friends might be right. Marriage certainly includes a lot more compromises than I expected.

Through riding friends of Nancy's, we learn of a nice two-bedroom house for rent on Beech Mill Road with five acres. When we check it out, we like what we see.

It's a nice, older house with a single car garage and a full, half above ground basement. The house has a big screened porch on one end and is shaded by a large beech tree on the other end. I guess there were lots of beech trees here once because of the street's name.

We like the area, too. Great Falls is a small village in an area that extends from Route 193 down to the Potomac River about a mile away. The region has gently rolling land covered with grassy fields and woods.

Sadly, the overriding feel of Great Falls is that of a rural area on the verge of transition. Some of the farms aren't being worked any more. Many houses look old and tired, but here and there, on a few subdivided farms, new construction is popping up.

The Beech Mill Road house we're looking at includes a fenced pasture in back which wraps around the far side of the house next door in an "L" shape and includes a pond next to the road. There's a section of woods at the back of the pasture. The owner's brother, Ted, who's a house painter, and his wife live in that next door house on the screened porch side.

The pasture is nice, but Nancy insists we need a barn. Luckily, the owner's cousins live across the street, and they have an empty four stall barn with an attached field and a small paddock.

The physical situation fits us perfectly. Me especially. The horses are close, but generally out of sight. They make us a great combined rental deal, and we agree.

While signing the rental agreement, it suddenly hits home that I'm getting married. My life is about to totally change. This is forever. Am I really ready for marriage?

The doubts churn in my head like bingo numbers in a rotating cage. I struggle to disregard them. I tell myself it's normal to have wedding jitters.

**

A month before the wedding we move our things into the house. Nancy gives up her apartment to save money and moves back in with her parents. She and Sharon ship the horses into the Great Falls barn and hang a sign that says Whimsey Hill Farm. That's the name they show Junior under.

Clarence and I will be living in the house for now. Clarence is the elderly groom from the Madeira school.

He moves into the basement of the house. He's been a good friend to Nancy and Sharon ever since Nancy's Madeira teaching days. He's offered to help with the horses in exchange for a room. Clarence is sixty plus. At this point, he's exhausted by a life of hard menial labor. Lately, he's been living out of his car. He's a hygienic underachiever, but a kind man. Who can say no when we have the space?

Nancy and I are happy, but tired when we finally take a break from unpacking boxes to sit out on the screened porch. Junior and Bear are turned out in the pasture behind the house. It's a late Sunday afternoon and the exceptionally hot, muggy day is draining our energy. We relax into some soft chairs to enjoy a cold soda.

I have to admit, I'm already loving the screened porch.

Nancy glances out toward the road. "Look," she says.

Cars are backed up bumper to bumper. It's an unusual occurrence on a street that sees maybe a few cars in a day. A few more cars stop, creating a miniscule traffic jam.

People step out of their cars and point toward the area near the pond. The pond is hidden from us by Ted's house, the trees and a dip in the field. The street goes right past it, and that seems to be where everyone is heading.

Has there been an accident? But people are laughing.

What the heck is going on?

Curiosity gets the best of us. We head out the front door and down the hill.

People are congregating at the fence next to the pond. Nancy and I work our way through the crowd.

As we get nearer, we laugh too. It's Junior. She's decided to cool off with a dip in the pond. But it's how she's doing it that has people in stitches.

Underwater in the pond, Junior lies upside down on her back. Only her nostrils and four hooves protrude above the surface. Her nostrils slowly inhale and exhale. That's the only sign she's alive. It's hysterical. She's totally oblivious to the crowd.

I'm starting to understand the expression - Junior is Junior.

By now, I've seen her do some pretty weird things. Like when Nancy goes out to catch her, Junior often runs behind a tree. But a whole horse is not an easy thing to hide and no tree in Virginia is big enough to cover Junior's rear end. The trunk covers her head, but all the rest of her hangs out behind in plain sight. Occasionally she'll peer out to locate Nancy and then jerk her head back quickly behind the tree. She always acts surprised when Nancy finds her.

No, that's not right. I misspoke. Horses don't get "surprised." I don't believe that animals have human characteristics.

Even so, thank goodness Junior doesn't have access to a lake. Having seen what she can do with a mud puddle and a pond, I shudder at the thought.

7

ONE PLUS ONE EQUALS SEVEN

The phone rings.

"Hi, honey." It's Nancy.

"Can you stick forty dollars in my checking account today?"

"Sure. Is everything all right?"

"Everything's fine."

"What's going on?"

"Long story. Tell you when I get home. Thanks, honey." Click.

Well, that was annoying. Could she have been any more cryptic?

It's the week after we moved our things into the Great Falls house. Nancy technically is living with her parents until the wedding, but she spends most of her time here.

She and Sharon left for a livestock sale this morning out near Winchester. They went to see what it's like. It isn't a fancy thoroughbred sale like Keeneland or Saratoga that auctions off expensive racehorses. This one is for local riding horses and farm horses.

Six hours after her call, Nancy comes in the door. She looks exhausted. I save my questions, hustle her into a hot tub with her favorite pine-scented bubble bath, and fix her a Coke with lots of ice and a slice of lemon, the way she likes it.

I turn on the living room television to watch my favorite show, *The Smothers Brothers*. As the final credits roll, Nancy emerges in her bathrobe to join me and talk about her day.

"Sharon and I were horrified by what went on. Some dealers bought and sold riding horses to livery stables, but several dealers purchased horses for meat companies or had contracts to send horses overseas for meat," she tells me.

"The place was terrible. It looked like it was made out of old lumber salvaged from the dump. The roof was low and everything was filthy and dingy. Horses were shoved into the auction ring, and all the dealers standing around cracked whips at the poor animals, scaring them to death. They seemed to think if the horse looked animated, it would sell better. It just seemed sadistic to me. The horses were nervous and frightened. Some were lame, old, and there was even one child's sweet, outgrown pony that was bought for meat.

"We left the sales ring and walked around in the barn area in back. In a tiny, dimly lit stall, we discovered a skinny, seventeen-hand, chestnut thoroughbred. He was so weak, he was leaning against the wall to stay upright. The roof was so low his withers brushed against the support beams. He had no food or water.

When I asked, a guy nearby told us the horse had already been sold to a meat company. We were appalled. The horse didn't look old and had a kind eye."

"I'm sorry you had to see that," I say.

"I don't know if he'll live through tonight."

"Try to think about something else."

"I'll be anxious until the vet sees him in the morning.

"Huh?"

"That's why I needed the money. We talked the meat buyer into selling him to us for forty dollars. Then we got him a ride as far as a friend's place. We weren't sure he'd make it. He can barely stand up."

"But you and Sharon already have horses."

"We'll get him healthy and then find him a good home. It won't cost anything to keep him because we have two empty stalls." I know there's got to be a hole in that logic big enough to drive a truck through, but I can't quite articulate it fast enough.

**

We drive out early the next morning to see the new horse. At the friend's barn, Sharon and Dr. Clark Harris, our veterinarian, both pull in right behind us. Dr. Clark, as he's known locally, is a warm, friendly man in his forties, who's taken care of Junior and Bear for several years.

He takes one look at the new horse and shakes his head. I do, too. Nancy's description last night didn't fully convey the terrible condition this poor animal is in.

Even a non-animal person like me is appalled by his protruding bones and stumbling movements.

Dr. Clark speaks first. "On top of everything else, it looks like he's been bled, poor fella."

"What does that mean?" I ask.

"Animal blood is sold to research labs. Greedy people take too much. They're squeezing the last nickel from what they feel is a useless horse."

Nancy and Sharon gasp.

Dr. Clark checks the horse over. When he finishes, he gives us a plan to slowly increase the horse's feed. Because of his weak condition, he can't handle too much initially. Dr. Clark gives him some shots and says he'll wait until he's stronger to worm him. He also tells us to wait a couple of days before we van him home.

Alarm bells join the "wedding is forever" doubts churning in my head.

We aren't even married yet, but we have a live-in groom, two horses, a dog, a house, a barn, a broken-down horse van, and now an additional broken-down horse - all on my Lieutenant's salary. I'm game, but I'm not a miracle worker.

8

SHE'S LATE, SHE'S LATE FOR A VERY IMPORTANT DATE

Our approaching wedding feels like a steam roller about to run us over. If Nancy has any second thoughts, she doesn't show it. Yet she seems withdrawn and unfocused at moments. When I call her on it, she shrugs it off.

By the day before the wedding, I'm on overload. My family, out of town relatives, and friends have been arriving all week. They all want to meet and talk. And there are still tons of decisions to be made.

The constant conflicts for my time make me feel yanked in two. Nancy's been at her parents for the last couple weeks. We haven't had any private time in ages. By the time the evening of the church rehearsal and the rehearsal dinner arrives, I'm tense and running on auto pilot. I just hope the smile plastered on my face successfully hides my fatigue from everyone.

I've been in several wedding parties, but I had no idea what it felt like to be the groom. People say weddings are a good test for marriages. I believe it because I've never been so stressed.

I arrive with my parents at Nancy's parents' house. We're to join them and Nancy for the drive to the church for the rehearsal and then on to the rehearsal dinner.

Only she's not there.

I'm stunned.

Her parents' concern shows on their faces. She was due an hour ago, and they haven't heard from her. It's 1968 - cell phones don't exist. Nancy gave up her CBS job, but she's spent the week covering for a friend who owns a professional boarding stable in McLean and is out of town. It's the same friend who took in our starving forty dollar horse overnight.

We're due at the church in just over an hour. My Naval training and personal inclination insist on punctuality. How dare she be late at such an important time? I'm totally embarrassed that it happens in front of my parents. I can only imagine what they're thinking.

We all sit in Nancy's parents' living room and sip coffee politely, trying to ignore the elephant in the room, "Where's Nancy?" Another half hour passes, and now I'm really worried. Why doesn't she call? Is she hurt? Should I drive out to the stable and find her? Anything could have happened. My anxiety grows.

I can't sit here politely anymore. I excuse myself and go outside to be alone. I pause to take deep breaths. It's odd how a situation like this makes all else in your life recede. I don't care about anything except that Nancy is okay.

Then out of the blue, my worst fear strikes me.

Has she changed her mind? Oh my God, have I been stood up? She's not coming back. She's decided not to marry me. The thought is devastating.

I hear a squeal of tires. Nancy's mother must have been

listening for it. She steps out of the house.

Nancy drives up in a rush. She pops out of her car. I can see she's covered in dirt and sweat. For the first time in our relationship, I yell at her before she can speak.

"Where on earth have you been?" It stops her cold. She looks at me with wounded eyes. I feel like a heel. I'm not a yeller by nature, and I'm not sure which of us is more surprised. But I hope never to see that stricken look on her face again. I stammer that I was worried.

At that point her Mother steps in and saves me.

"Brad, why don't you take your parents on to the church and let everyone know we'll be a few minutes late." She whisks Nancy away to the shower before either of us can get a word in.

I dutifully gather my parents and head for the church. They are full of unspoken questions. I catch the glances and raised eyebrows between them. Luckily, the short drive is silent. My mother pats me comfortingly on the arm as we enter the church. That only makes me worry more.

The wedding party happily chatters while we wait, but I feel totally disconnected from everything. My brain is in turmoil. Ten minutes later, Nancy and her parents hurry in. The rushed rehearsal goes by in a blur.

Surrounded by people, Nancy and I have no time to talk. I recognize the expression on her face as the same glued-on smile I've been wearing lately. Is it possible she's questioning our marriage too? When the rehearsal is over and everyone piles into cars heading for the rehearsal dinner, we manage to grab a few minutes alone.

"I'm so sorry I was late," she begins.

"I'm sorry I yelled. I didn't know what to think."

"My friend was expecting a new horse named Dasher to be delivered this morning. The truck didn't show up until I was closing up the barn to come home. The horse was skittish when it was unloaded.

The van driver handed its lead shank to one of the kids from the barn. Then he slammed the truck's door. Dasher spooked and yanked the lead shank right out of the kid's hand. The horse bolted down the driveway and straight up the new Dulles Access Road."

The Dulles Airport Access Road, which is going to connect McLean to Dulles International Airport, is a six lane, twelve mile long stretch of highway currently under construction. At this time, it's graded, but not paved. Nancy's friend's stable is right where the Dulles highway meets Route 123, the main McLean bypass road.

"It was after four o'clock," she continues. "The road construction workers were gone for the day.

I asked the van driver for help, but he leapt into his truck and drove away. I was the only adult there. So I took off after the horse on foot.

Panicked by the unfamiliar location, Dasher hit the wide, level Dulles road and kept on going. He must have thought he was on the racetrack to end all racetracks. I managed to keep him in sight. I knew if he got out on a regular street and was hit by a car, people could be hurt, even killed! I would be responsible. When I was in high school, my friend's pony broke loose. He got out on the highway and ended up through the windshield of a truck. It was terrible. I had to catch that horse."

I swallow my ego. Of course she did. She was right.

"It took me five miles and a sprint between some trees after the horse finally veered off. Exhausted and disoriented, he finally slowed. There wasn't an animal, house, or person in sight except me.

He let me approach and catch the lead shank. Then I had to lead him all the way back. He cooled down by then, but was covered in dried sweat. I had to hose him down and leave a note for my friend about what happened."

"Whoever named him Dasher had a sense of humor."

We hug and kiss. I vow to never yell at her again.

The smiles on our faces are genuine as we leave for the rehearsal dinner.

Tomorrow is the big day.

9

WHAT'S COOKING?

When you're newlyweds, it's a big deal when your folks come to visit for the first major holiday.

My parents are snowbirds. They pass through Virginia on their yearly winter trek from their current home in New Hampshire to Florida. They'll arrive tomorrow - Thanksgiving morning, stay overnight, and leave at dawn the next morning. We haven't seen them since our wedding six months ago.

Nancy and I both have warm memories of holiday dinners while growing up.

The preparations, the special family recipes, and the relaxed, "I ate too much" conversation afterwards. Now it's our turn to be the adults and host the dinner.

We wash our wedding china and wine glasses in preparation. We make up the guest bedroom, clean the bathroom, and collect extra chairs to use in the dining room. There is only one problem.

Nancy can't cook.

Who knew?

Apparently, her mother never taught her to make anything

except pie crust and cookies. Even with those, she didn't get to do them totally. Her mother, a perfectionist, always had to prepare food exactly the way she wanted it, so there was no room for the errors of a beginner.

I do remember one night when we were at the dinner table at Nancy's parents, I noticed her mother picking the mushrooms out of the chicken casserole she had made and served.

"Don't you like mushrooms," I asked.

"No."

"Then why don't you leave them out?"

"I can't do that. The recipe calls for them." Hmmm. Not an intuitive cook. Maybe there was a reason Nancy avoided the kitchen.

Regardless, I can't get over Nancy not being able to cook. She lived in an apartment with a roommate for years before we married.

I have to ask her, "What did you eat?"

"I didn't have to cook," she explains. "When a guy asked me out, it was usually for dinner. Then I'd bring home a doggie bag for either me or my roommate. My roommate did the same thing. We once went two months without buying any food and still ate two meals a day. Which was good, because there wasn't enough money in my paycheck to buy food for me, Junior, and Amy and have enough left over to pay entry fees for horse shows."

Okay. That's honest, just not the reason I expected to hear.

I guess I've been missing the signs. All the dinners she'd made since we married consist of soup, chili, mac and cheese, and hot dogs. Anything that can be prepared from a can and then served with cookies. Lots of cookies. Especially our absolute favorite, chocolate chip cookies. Looking back, I realize that I had cooked all the meals that started from scratch.

But I can see the determination in Nancy to make Thanksgiving dinner on her own. She starts prepping bravely. It only takes four long distance phone calls to her mother in Arlington and three cookbooks for reference, to complete a homemade pumpkin pie.

Come to think of it, we did get a lot of cookbooks for wedding presents. Maybe I should have paid more attention to the implied message.

It's late by the time Nancy finally places the pie in the refrigerator to chill overnight.

I have to laugh thinking of Nancy sweating about making a pie, when hurtling over jumps on a horse never gives her pause.

To be fair, she warned me before we married, "I don't do domestic." At the time, I was amused. Now I'm finding she was being deadly serious. The barn, her tack, and the animals are immaculate, the house...not so much.

"Why isn't the house the same as the barn in your thinking?" I ask.

"There's only so much time in life," she explains. "And I don't want to spend mine cleaning house." That's totally opposite my upbringing, my training in the Navy, and my natural inclination. I'm not sure what to think. Luckily, she considers our relationship important.

But there is one domestic thing she likes to do. She likes to paint. That's paint as in room walls, not as on canvas. Her major in school was art, so painting on canvas and drawing cartoons are normal pastimes for her. I'm not sure where liking to paint rooms comes from. I unhappily discovered this interest just last week.

I came home from work to find Nancy sprinkled in blue

paint.

Her explanation?

"Since your parents are coming, I decided to paint the kitchen. The old cream color was too dull."

I look at the kitchen in shock. "Where did you get the paint?"

"I found it down in the basement. I figured I only needed a gallon to do the job," she said. "I found a half a gallon of white and a half a gallon of a medium blue. So I thought light blue would make a great color for the kitchen. I poured the two half gallons together and stirred." I notice the paint cans in the trash.

"Have any problems?" I ask cautiously.

"Well, it seemed pretty frothy. And when I put it on the walls, it was kind of thick and bumpy. I've never painted with textured paint before. I just finished. Didn't it come out great?"

"Great" isn't quite what I would have called it. Frothy yes, great no.

I reach over and touch the wall in disbelief. Nancy has mixed a half a can of latex paint with half a can of oil-based paint. The 'texture' she likes is caused by air bubbles since oil and water-based latex paint wouldn't mix. It gives the walls and the moldings a sharp, pointy, irregular surface.

Somehow she's managed to stir the paints so thoroughly that at least the color is consistent. I didn't even know that was possible.

I sputter appreciative noises and excuse myself. I have to get out of the kitchen before I say something I'll regret.

Next time Nancy goes riding, I warn the landlord's brother next door about the kitchen paint. The one that's a professional housepainter. He insists on seeing the kitchen for himself.

The look on his stunned face will be etched in my memory

forever. He staggers out of our house and back over to his without a word.

I have a feeling that when we move out, we won't be getting our security deposit back. Someone is going to have to sand the paint off the entire kitchen before it can be repainted.

I'm not sure how I'll explain the paint to my parents. There's absolutely no way to hide it.

Nancy works out Thanksgiving dinner carefully, trying to keep it simple. We'll use canned cranberries and frozen green beans. But there was no getting around cooking the turkey, stuffing, mashed potatoes, and gravy.

She also writes a detailed schedule for us for tonight and tomorrow to post in the kitchen. That only takes six more calls to her Mother.

Nancy meticulously calculates the timing of the food in and out of the oven so it will all land on the table simultaneously at five o'clock. In addition, she has to merge in the horses' schedules. I know she's feeling the pressure, but she won't let me help with anything but the side dishes.

Thanksgiving eve stretches on forever. We had not counted on how much work is involved. Our own mothers made it look effortless. Even with two of us, every time we check an item off the "to do" list, two more get added.

We finally get to bed late. The day's list has been accomplished. Tomorrow's list awaits. The turkey defrosts in the refrigerator overnight. Yet sleep doesn't happen.

Nancy gets up again. She moves over to sit by the second floor bedroom window.

"What are you doing, honey?" I mumble.

"The moon's bright tonight. I love the shadow patterns that

the beech tree's branches make below on the grass. They're so beautiful, it's always calming. Like being near the ocean, the timelessness of it puts things in perspective."

I put on my slippers and check out what she's seeing. She's right. The beech tree at the end of the house is large and round. The moon lights up the yard and with the leaves all gone, the intricate branch shadows are fascinating.

"Come on, honey." I get her to return to bed.

"I want tomorrow to be perfect for your parents," she whispers as she drifts off to sleep spooned against me.

I reassure her, "It will be, honey. Don't worry. And if it isn't, that's okay too." My eyes close, and I peacefully drift off to sleep, believing everything is under control.

10

A FOWL DAY

The early light coming in the window wakes me. I glance outside. The light frost on the ground will melt quickly as the sun rises. A perfect day for Thanksgiving. Crisp and sunny.

Fall is her favorite time of year, Nancy says. Nights cool enough for the fireplace and days cool enough for sweaters. It might become my favorite time of year too. I don't care much for wearing sweaters, but I certainly enjoy watching them on Nancy.

I catch myself whistling as I shower and shave. Life is good.

I'm making coffee in our blue kitchen when Nancy, back from the barn, charges through the kitchen. Never a coffee drinker, she grabs a Coke from the refrigerator, and heads to wash up.

I have omelets ready when she returns. Over breakfast, we run through the day's list. First up is Nancy's popular family recipe for blue cheese dip with crackers and veggies that will serve as the appetizer. I'll prep the veggies, and Nancy will make the dip. On completion, dip and veggies will go into the refrigerator until needed. Then I'll start cooking and chopping chestnuts and celery for the stuffing. Nancy will prep the turkey and stuff it when I'm done. Later we'd deal with the gravy, mashed potatoes, cranberries, and green beans. Wine and apple cider are already in the refrigerator cooling.

That leaves setting the table and the evening round with the horses. We have our game plan ready. We're good to go.

Before we finish breakfast, my parents arrive. Nancy settles them in the guest room and I make another round of omelets. It's noon when Nancy and I move into the kitchen to start the dinner. My parents are resting. So far we're right on schedule.

I glance out the window. The forty-dollar horse Nancy and Sharon rescued from the killers, now nicknamed Skinny, is turned out in the pasture behind the house. He's become very popular with our friends who sympathize with his sad story. Several of them go so far as to bring him treats when visiting. He accepts it all with quiet dignity.

He's truly a gentle giant.

But now he's rolling on the ground oddly. By this time, I've seen all the horses roll, get up, and shake themselves off. But this is different. Skinny keeps rolling. And he's biting his sides.

"Nancy, come look at Skinny."

She joins me at the window. "Oh, no!"

I follow as she races out back.

"He's got colic."

"What?" She rushes out to Skinny and snaps the lead shank on his halter while dodging his flailing hooves.

"Help me," she yells. "We have to get him up." I have no idea why she's upset, but clearly she is. I hurry to help her.

We manage to force Skinny to his feet, but, in spite of our efforts, he keeps trying to lie down again. Nancy and I keep prodding and pushing until we get him to start walking.

"Call Dr. Clark. Ask him to come as soon as he can," she says. "Tell him it's colic. Bad."

I charge into the house for the phone.

I learn later that horses are physically incapable of vomiting, unlike dogs and humans. Anything they swallow or any gas can only exit out through the rear end.

If there's a blockage in the intestines, a horse feels acute pain and will lie down and roll. When the horse rolls, his intestine can become twisted. If that happens, nothing can get out. The blockage is permanent and can only be relieved by an operation or the horse will die. Frequently they die even with an operation.

Keeping a horse moving and on its feet is one way to prevent a twisted intestine, if it hasn't occurred yet, until the vet comes. Sometimes a horse will have a bowel movement and relieve the pressure himself. The longer the intestines remain blocked, the more chance of losing the horse.

I grab the phone and start dialing. Dr. Clark's number is right beside the phone.

Bad news. He's away. His recording gives another vet's number to call for emergencies. I dial it. His recording answers and says leave a message. I do so and run back out to Nancy.

"Call Dr. Williamson or Dr. Simmons in Fairfax," she suggests as she and Skinny continue walking.

When I return to the house, my parents are up. I explain the problem as I hunt for the phone numbers. They offer to help, but there's really nothing they can do.

I have no luck with Dr. Williamson, or with Dr. Simmons, but Dr. Simmons' office refers me to a Dr. Kaudner. His clinic answers. Dr. Kaudner will come as soon as he can, but he's setting

51

a dog's broken leg at the moment. I hurry back to Nancy with the news.

"We have a vet, but we don't know when he'll get here." She's exhausted. I grab Skinny's lead shank and force her to sit. At least I can give her a break. She collapses on the ground. Skinny tries to lie down, too, but I prod him like I saw Nancy do and manage to keep him on his feet and moving. I don't know what we'll do if he gets down and we can't get him up again. I can see the stress in Nancy's face.

"I'm so sorry about your parents. Thanksgiving is totally ruined."

Yeah, I'm not happy either. I keep walking.

The next time I pass near Nancy, she says, "They must think I'm crazy." Right then, my parents come out to see what's going on.

Nancy apologizes about the neglected dinner and tries to explain about colic.

"We have to keep walking him until the veterinarian arrives."

I feel terrible. I can tell my parents don't understand. They nod graciously and head back inside, but I can see they're hurt. I give Skinny to Nancy and follow my parents. It's hard to explain why walking the horse is important. I'm not sure they understand either.

Nancy and I settle take turns leading Skinny every twenty minutes. At one point, I catch myself patting Skinny and telling him everything will be okay. I had to laugh at myself for fearlessly touching him, but who could be afraid of poor Skinny, stumbling along in pain.

Every couple of trades I call Dr. Kaudner's office. At last they tell me he's on his way. Relief.

Soon, Dr. Kaudner pulls in the driveway. He confirms the horse has serious colic. He quickly gets to work. He inserts a tube into Skinny's nostril and down into his stomach, and gives him a lubricant through it. Then he gives him a shot of a muscle relaxer. In his hands, Skinny's intestines clear and he recovers. Luckily it was a blockage and not a twisted intestine.

According to the vet, "Untreated colic can be deadly. It's the leading cause of death in horses."

We feel immense relief that Skinny's okay.

By the time Dr. Kaudner leaves it's past seven o'clock at night. I have to say, I've never been so happy to see a horse poop in my life. It means Skinny's blockage has cleared and we are done with the walking.

This is not the special first Thanksgiving I'd imagined with my family. To be honest, I'm unhappy.

Thoroughly drained, Nancy and I head for the house with more apologies on our lips. Maybe we can make sandwiches and salvage some time with my parents.

We stop in our tracks as we enter the kitchen.

There's a wonderful aroma of turkey cooking.

"What...?" My mother looks up from the stove and sees our surprise.

"Dinner in twenty minutes," she says. "I saw the menu posted in the kitchen. So I just followed it. After you wash up, why don't you pour us all some wine?"

I'm relieved and ecstatic. We're going to have a Thanksgiving dinner with my Mom and Dad. What a glorious end to an awful day.

Nancy and I are half way to the bathroom when I hear my Mom add, "I love what you've done with the kitchen. I've heard about the new textured paints, but this is the first time I've ever seen it."

11

ALONG CAME A SPYDER

Our one year anniversary approaches. The time has come to make the "BIG" decision.

This morning, breakfast consists the usual choice of Cheerios, Kix, or Puffed Wheat. Nancy hasn't learned to cook oatmeal, eggs, or bacon yet. She figured out French toast and found a great family recipe for waffles, but who can eat a steady diet of maple syrup without rotting their teeth and gaining a thousand pounds? Good thing I make my own coffee.

I glance up from my morning newspaper and notice Nancy concentrating on the new copy of *Cosmopolitan* magazine. In fact, she has a pencil in her hand and seems to be writing on the page.

"Interesting?" I ask.

Startled, she quickly flips the page. "Just a silly article. I'm going to turn the horses out," she says and leaves carrying the magazine.

Odd reaction.

I put down the paper and concentrate on the decision I have to make.

My current project, developing control systems that let robots and computers work together in automated factories, is going well and getting notice.

The horses happily eat away in their barn across the street. Just far enough away that I don't have to deal with them. We arrived with two horses, Junior and Sharon's Bear. Then came Skinny.

But I've learned a hard lesson. Nancy, like nature, abhors a vacuum. The barn has four stalls so she needs four horses to fill them.

Nancy and Sharon attended a second livestock sale a little while ago. This time they rescued a starving dark brown mare from the killers.

They name her Spyder and call her a treasure. She looks like another hungry, thin horse to me. Nancy says Spyder is gentle and sweet with one interesting characteristic. When you say "Whoa," she stops dead. By dead stop, I mean like going thirty miles an hour and hitting a brick wall kind of stop.

Nancy convinces me she's so quiet, I should try riding her. She even rides Spyder and demonstrates. It's true. She always stops when you say "Whoa." I cautiously agree.

At the appointed time, I arrive across the street at the barn. Spyder is tacked up and waiting with Nancy. Clarence sits in the barn door to watch. After a bit of coaching, I manage to scramble into the saddle.

Somehow horses seem a lot taller when you're trying to get on one. Once you get up there, it looks like a long way down, too.

I can see Clarence snickering out of the corner of my eye. Maybe this wasn't such a hot idea.

Nancy leads me around in a circle explaining the use of the

reins. Okay. I relax.

I can do this. Right rein to go right, left rein to go left. Two reins together and back to stop. I didn't realize the steering controls were so easy.

"Would you like to try a trot?" Nancy asks after a bit.

"Sure, why not." I'm feeling pretty cocky.

Big mistake. When Clarence moves to get a better view, I should have been warned.

Spyder trots with Nancy leading her.

Not good. I try, but I get totally out of sync with the motion. I find myself bouncing like a rubber ball attached by a rubber band to a ping pong paddle.

No way can I find my balance.

"Whoa!" jolts out of me.

Blam! Dead stop. If Spyder didn't have a long neck, I would have been on the ground. Wow. I'm ecstatic. She stopped when I asked. I could like this horse.

"Are you okay?"

"Fine." I answer, failing to mention I'm going to be walking funny for a week.

"I think that's enough for now."

Clarence disappears into the barn. A strange noise erupts from inside. "Hawp, hawp, hawp." I realize it's the sound of Clarence laughing.

I choose to ignore him.

Nancy shows me how to dismount by taking both feet out of the stirrups and sliding down the left side of the horse. I've seen her do this gracefully countless times.

Not so for me. My knees buckle when they hit the ground. I sprawl in a tangled heap at Spyder's side.

"Hawp, hawp, hawp."

**

A few weeks later, Nancy takes a call from a man in Maryland looking for a horse as a surprise present for his daughter.

"I want something safe and quiet so she'll enjoy riding," he said.

Nancy tells him about Spyder. Interested, he arrives the next day. He's in his forties, tall, athletic, and seems like a nice guy. I go along with them to the barn.

He tacks Spyder up himself to do a test ride. It seems that buyers do that for horses just like they do for cars. Hopefully horses don't get their legs kicked like tires do.

Nancy warns the man about Spyder's four-wheel disc brakes, yet from where I'm watching, I can tell he isn't paying much attention to her words.

Okay. I'm guilty. I want to see what happens when he says "Whoa." Then I can join Clarence and go "Hawp. Hawp." I notice Clarence keeping an eye on things from near the barn. He and I grin and exchange a wink.

The man rides Spyder for about fifteen minutes before he breathes "Whoa." Even though he says it softly, it still has the same effect on Spyder. Full dead stop. The man rides well, so it doesn't catch him like it did me, but he's definitely surprised.

Clarence and I are disappointed. We'd hoped for more of a show.

The man glances at Nancy. "She does that every time?"

"Every time we say the word," she laughs.

He smiles and rides a few more minutes. When he dismounts, he pats Spyder.

"I'll take her. I won't worry about my daughter when she's

riding her. No matter what happens, she only has to say 'Whoa.' She's perfect." He works out the details with Nancy. She's surprised when he waives the customary vet check. Veterinarians give horses a physical when they change hands. Just the way a smart car buyer has his own mechanic check under the hood.

The man does have a request. He wants us to keep Spyder until the night before his daughter's birthday in two weeks.

**

On the appointed evening, Nancy and I deliver Spyder to her new home. The trip is over an hour and a half away.

I'm more than a bit impressed when we arrive even though it's dark. The barn is as nice as our house. Spyder's stall at home is twelve feet by ten feet. Her new one has to be at least twenty foot square and so immaculate I could have lived in it. The straw is at least two feet deep.

Nancy takes our blanket off and her new owner puts on a brand new, expensive looking one. Then he puts a beautiful leather halter on her with her name on it. Spyder has landed in a good place. Even I leave with a warm feeling.

On the way home, Nancy claims, "You could almost hear Spyder sigh. Can you imagine? A short while ago she was headed for the meat market, and now she's living in horse heaven with people who are going to love her. Could it get any better?" I begin to understand why Nancy enjoys rescuing horses.

Our pleasure doesn't last long. On the way home, the decrepit old van dies on the busy 495 Beltway that circles D.C., parts of Maryland, and Virginia. We barely manage to roll to the shoulder before it stops dead.

An hour later, the weary, local mechanic on night duty declares from under the hood, "It needs a new engine."

Horror registers on Nancy's face. "Sharon and I put in a new motor already."

I know she's upset. Still, I think to myself, this rattle trap van should have been retired ages ago, but Sharon and Nancy were happy with it.

"How much?" Nancy queries.

"At least five hundred dollars." Ouch.

I make arrangements for the van to be towed and tell the mechanic, "Thank you for all your help. We'll call in the morning with a decision."

So now there are two big decisions to make. What to do with the van and did I really want to continue to live in the country? I had some ideas about the van, but not a clue about the other.

After breakfast the next morning, I head out to our screened porch to think.

As I pass through the living room, I notice the *Cosmopolitan* Nancy had been reading in the trash can. I retrieve it with the intention of idly flipping through it.

Settling into a porch chair, I glance at it. There's a sexy woman in a hot outfit on the cover. Looking down, I notice the feature article, "Are You and Your Mate Compatible?" Is that what Nancy was looking at? Of course we're compatible. Does she have any doubts? I don't need a magazine article to answer that question.

Still, I'm curious to see what they say. I flip to the article.

There are pencil marks in the answer boxes. It is what she was reading. I turn to the results page.

There, in black and white, the article determined that Nancy and I are "Highly Incompatible." That can't be true. Is it what Nancy thinks?

I slam the magazine right back in the trash.

Then I remember. She called it "Silly." I agree. Stupid and silly. What do they know?

12

MAY THE HORSE BE WITH YOU

"So," Nancy asks anxiously, "the year is up. Have you decided if you want to continue living in the country?"

There it is, finally out on the table.

Nancy's been nervous all week and trying very unsuccessfully to hide it. Every night she attempts to cook a good dinner with varying results. Anywhere from poor to inedible. Luckily she's been serving my favorite Merlot with meals. A little alcohol can cover a lot of sins. Having Amy under the table to gobble up tidbits when Nancy's not looking helps too.

Ironing is next to cooking on Nancy's list of under-developed skills. She washes clothes well, but the ironing board doesn't come out until the clean laundry pile takes over our bedroom. It's not a thing that bothers me. Luckily, I have no aversion to picking up an iron if necessary.

When I came home today, I found all my work shirts neatly ironed and hung in the closet. Definitely a first.

I know this is a short-term thing until I make my decision. Still, all this "attention" to my needs is feeling weird. So much so that I feel like patting Nancy on the head and saying, "Good girl."

We dress in our best for our first anniversary dinner. Even Amy wears a big white bow. Our wedding china and the two dozen red roses I've given Nancy create a warm mood at the table.

Later, the tall vanilla-scented candles burn low in their glass holders. The special filet mignon steaks are gone. The bottle of my favorite Merlot is reduced to a final half a glass each. As the evening comes to a mellow end, I'm feeling so content, I even catch myself absently petting Amy.

But Nancy's worry has been the elephant in the room all night.

She repeats her question. "Have you decided if you want to continue living in the country?"

"Before we talk about that, I'd like you to open your gift." She hesitates, then accepts the small gift-wrapped box I pull from my pocket.

Inside she finds a key.

She gives me a surprised look. "What's this for?"

"It's a surprise." I stand and reach for her hand. "Let's walk over to the barn." As soon as we're close, she spots my present. A used pickup truck with a used Rice two-horse trailer is parked in front of the barn. Her face lights up.

I tell her, "If you like it, we'll need to turn in your Volkswagen to the dealer tomorrow." The hugs and kisses I receive assure me she likes it very much.

I'm relieved she does. I'm much happier with the thought of Nancy and Sharon no longer driving around in that old rattle trap van. There were moments when I fought the urge to take a match to it.

The pickup and trailer are my present to her, but, honestly, the relief is a present to me. This is one bill I'll pay happily.

Go forth and rescue horses safely, I think, remembering Spyder's happy ending.

Later, as we're headed for bed, I answer Nancy's question. Yes, I like living in the country. I'm surprised myself. I enjoy the peace and quiet after a day of turmoil at work. I like the fresh, clean air and the open space.

What I don't say is, if one could live in the country without animals, it might be Shangri-La.

Luckily our first year of marriage has taught me to choose my words carefully.

13

YOU CAN LEAD A HORSE TO WATER...

Nancy's sick.

She has a fever, can't keep food down, and has no energy.

We went to her parents' doctor, who keeps prescribing medications for what he calls a bad virus. He says she'll be over it in a couple weeks, but every day feels like an eon to me.

I'm worried because she doesn't seem to be getting better. If anything she's getting sicker.

We've been married just over a year, and this is the first time either of us has had anything more than a cold. As I leave for work in the morning, Nancy sleeps restlessly in the downstairs bedroom so she can be closer to our only bathroom. When I return at the end of the day, she's still there. Amy rarely leaves her side.

Clarence comes home on his lunch hour and checks in on her. He promises to call me if she gets worse. I can't accomplish much at work because of my concern.

Then there's a related problem. Clarence feeds and cleans stalls, but he has arthritic knees and hands from years of heavy labor. I know that makes it painful for him if the horses jerk him around when he leads them. It also prevents him from being able to hold onto them if they get frisky.

Nancy apologizes for asking me to help Clarence by taking the horses in and out, but I know there's nobody else. I assure her I can do this. I definitely don't want to, but I can. After all, I did lead Skinny around at Thanksgiving.

"A sick, exhausted horse is not the same as a healthy, bouncy one," Nancy reminds me.

"Hey. I went to college. I can lead a couple of horses." She's too ill to argue, but I can see she's worried. She instructs me carefully on their routine. Apparently there's a specific pecking order involved. Junior first, then Bear and then Skinny. Supposedly all hell breaks loose if the order gets changed - a possibility I have no intention of testing.

Luckily for me, the horses only have to go about seventy-five feet from their stalls to their pasture. I just don't want Nancy getting up and trying to do it herself.

This leading from the barn to the field takes place twice a day. Out to the field in the morning and back into the barn in the evening.

My bravado disappears on the first morning as soon as I hook the lead shank to Junior's halter.

"It's only seventy-five feet, it's only seventy-five feet," I repeat over and over to myself. "Nancy does this every day. I can too." I hold the lead shank like Nancy taught me. Right hand near the halter, left hand gripping the extra part of the lead. I try to remember all of Nancy's instructions.

"Never, never wrap any part of the lead rope over your shoulder, around your hand or any other part of your body. If the horse moves suddenly, the lead could pull tight and you could be dragged." As being dragged is something I hope to avoid at all costs, I follow Nancy's instructions to the letter.

The morning passes without a hitch. I'm quite pleased with myself. How pathetic is that? Proud because I can lead horses seventy-five feet? I wouldn't call it the best use of my abilities.

Turning the horses out each day gives me a closer look at the functions of the barn. I never realized how labor intensive the work is. None of it appears hard, it's just repetitive, tedious, and time consuming.

The horses each get totally different amounts of food and vitamins. Two drink lots of water and one doesn't. But since horses can't operate the water spigot and fill their own buckets when needed, they need to be checked frequently.

Junior, what a surprise, likes to 'wash' her food like a raccoon and regularly dunks her mouth full of food in her bucket. Half of her food ends up in the bottom. That means the water is dirty and needs to dumped and refilled even more often.

I find myself mulling over the problem while I'm at my office. There has to be an easier way to do all this routine work.

And then it hits me! Repetitive work is what I create robots to do. Who better than me to design a solution?

I work feverishly through my lunch hour. What I need is some sort of tank for each horse that can be pre-loaded with the individual animal's meals. The tanks will need a timer of some sort to let it drop the food into the horse's feed bucket at meal times. Piece of cake.

After working out the design, I stop at the hardware store on the way home.

Next, I go to Southern States, our local farmers' co-op. They handle things like different livestock feeds, gardening tools, fencing, farm supplies and equipment parts.

Owen, the clerk there, gets interested in my project. He grew up on a big farm and understands how useful my idea is and the basic mechanics of how it will work. He helps me find the remaining things I need.

"I can't imagine why no one's done this before," I say.

"Sure would save a lot of time," Owen responds in his thick country drawl.

"I'm going to work on the water problem next."

Owen thinks a minute. "You know, I think I saw something like automatic waterers out back. Hang on a minute while I check."

Great, someone else has already solved that problem. That will save me a lot of time.

Across the store, Owen chats with Archie, the manager. Archie shoots me an odd look and then says some more to Owen while shaking his head.

Owen rejoins me. "I was right. There are individual automatic waterers out back.

"Great. Let's see them."

"Archie doesn't recommend them."

"Why not?"

"Seems he ordered them for a big thoroughbred breeding outfit in Middleburg.

They used the waterers for a month and then pulled them all out and told us to resell them if we could."

"But they worked, right?"

"Archie says they function perfectly. Doesn't make any sense to him."

"Let's look at them."

Owen locates the waterers in the back of the building behind stacks of fence posts and partially under a pile of aluminum farm gates.

Just looking at them, I can tell they're great. Made of metal, each waterer has a shallow bowl with a plunger at the bottom. Someone has come up with a really smart concept.

When thirsty, a horse reaches for the small amount of water that sits at the bottom under the plunger. The horse has to push the plunger with its nose to reach the water. The light push on the plunger allows water to flow into the bowl and stops when the horse releases it to drink. And they only require a small amount of plumbing.

Perfect. I buy four of them after a little haggling because they're used. Owen kindly throws in a book on basic plumbing, which saves me a trip to the library.

It'll be a nice surprise for Nancy. I'm not going to tell her until I get everything installed over the weekend. I do confide in Clarence that night, though.

He shakes his head, "Don't seem right, somehow."

I try to explain how it will save time, but he's not convinced. I let it go. Nancy will understand.

By Thursday, Nancy's still not improving and I'm getting even more anxious. I call the Main Navy Medical office, down on the mall in Washington, D.C. for an appointment. It's time for a second opinion.

The next day I take her in. The circles under her eyes are deeper and the exhaustion is apparent when she moves. The doctor says he doesn't think it's a virus, but won't say what until he gets the test results back from the lab. He'll call us on Monday and tells us to try not to worry over the weekend.

That's easier said than done, but the feeder and waterer

projects help keep my mind occupied. I decide to move Junior's waterer as far away from her feed bucket as possible. Maybe she'll feel less of an urge to wash everything if she has to go farther.

Clarence stops me. He says it's good when horses wash their food. They ingest less dust and dirt. Reluctantly, I move Junior's waterer back near the feed bucket.

By Sunday evening, I finally get everything working. I explain it all to Clarence, but he's still skeptical.

I set the timers for the feeders for the horses' dinner that night. We watch as the food drops into the appropriate feed buckets at the appointed time. Clarence actually looks impressed.

I help Clarence reload the feeders for breakfast and dinner the next day. He's still not happy about leaving the horses without traditional water buckets.

"Does Nancy know about no buckets?"

"Not yet. It's a surprise." I go over again how the waterers work. I point out that Bear, who Nancy and Sharon often call DumDum because he's actually as smart as a whip, has figured it out and is drinking from his already.

Clarence goes silent as we close up the barn for the night.

**

Monday morning, I pop over to the barn. I'm happily humming as I anticipate showing Clarence how well my automatic systems worked. In fact, I'm forming an idea for my next creation.

Why not have a pulley arrangement going from the barn to the field? You could hook up the horses to it at the barn, turn it on and it would lead the horses out to the field. Once there, a remote control could be pressed that would release the horses.

Presto! With this system, even Clarence could send the horses out to the field. Of course, I'll need to create another remote to open and close the gate. That one has me a bit stumped.

As I approach the barn, I can hear, "Hawp! Hawp! Hawp! I wonder what's amusing Clarence?

I enter the barn, nod good morning to Clarence, and glance around for the source of his amusement.

"Oh, no!" I'm up to my ankles in water. The entire barn is flooded.

Clarence points at one of the horses.

Junior.

Who else?

As we watch, she presses the plunger in the waterer. She holds it down and doesn't release the plunger as the bowl fills, even though her nostrils disappear under water. The water overflows the bowl and cascades to the floor.

I guess she found a way to make her own puddle. She must have been playing with it all night to create such a mess.

The barn is full of floating straw and poop. Then I notice two of the feeder tanks are gone. I locate them floating in Junior's and Bear's stalls. The horses have broken them open and the grain for their dinner bobbles in the water and muck.

"Hawp! Ha --"

The look I give him cuts Clarence off mid-Hawp.

I swear him to secrecy. Nancy doesn't need to know about this. I decide it's not a good time to introduce my barn-to-field pulley idea, either.

Bailing the barn and removing the waterers makes me three hours late to work.

That means I'll have to give up my lunch hour and stay late tonight to make up the time.

I was never late before we moved to the farm. Now it's

happening too often. My boss hasn't said anything yet, but I'm starting to get disapproving glances. It's only a matter of time until it affects my job.

On the way home, I stop at Southern States, drop off our waterers and ask Owen to resell them. Like the breeding farm people from Middleburg, I don't hang around to discuss it.

As I finally pull in our driveway, I wonder if the reason the breeding farm returned the waterers was because they had a Junior of their own. No, that's not possible. There can't be two horses like her.

I'm surprised when Nancy greets me at the door.

"The Navy doctor called."

Oh my God. I'd totally forgotten. "What did he say?"

She smiles, "We're pregnant."

14

THAT SINKING FEELING

Nancy's miserable-vomiting for two to three hours every morning, and only able to eat a single cracker. Trying to have a conversation with her before she munches on that cracker is dangerous. After that she feels fine. I'm not sure I could deal with a routine like that, but she seems okay with it.

Looking back, I have a hard time understanding how a doctor wouldn't at least suspect pregnancy in a young couple married just over a year. Not that we guessed either, but we're not in the medical profession.

A pregnant wife is certainly better than a wife who's ill with an unknown virus.

We enjoy sharing the happy news with friends and family.

It's also with a sense of relief when I'm able to hand the barn duties back to Nancy.

I've accepted that my wife is no domestic goddess, but I don't know what I expected after we learned about the baby. Maybe that Nancy would abandon her "I don't do domestic" mantra, think more about the coming baby, and forget about the horses. I should have known better. Sometimes she shops for cutsie baby clothes, but otherwise there's no change in her routine.

That's not to say she's totally uninvolved. The doctor has laid out a program for her and she follows it strictly. With his approval, she resumes her full horse activities including riding.

I'm the one nervously reading Dr. Benjamin Spock's books on raising babies.

**

By now, Skinny is almost unrecognizable. He soon finds a good home with a tall woman who's looking for a quiet pleasure horse. It's with real remorse that I watch him leave. He and Spyder were my only barn buddies. Bear makes me nervous and Junior scares the bejeezus out of me.

Skinny's stall isn't vacant for long. The next resident is a thoroughbred mare from another auction. The front of the mare's face looks like someone had split it up between the eyes with an axe and it healed with no medical attention. Two enormous parallel ridges of lumpy scar tissue run at a slight diagonal from above her nostrils to her ears. It's a horrific sight. That she's skin and bone is a given. They name her Sweet Charity.

"Even when she's fatter, who's going to buy a horse that looks like that?" I have to ask. All I can think of is money thrown down the drain. Money we should be saving for the new baby.

Nancy shrugs. "She has a nice body, and doesn't she just break your heart?"

"You're changing the subject."

"I admit it will be hard, but we couldn't leave her." What could I say? There's no way we can ask the meat packers for our money back even if Nancy would let me. Another glance at Charity's awful face and I knew I couldn't send her to such a fate

76

either.

**

Two months later, I'm deep into the schematics on my current project at work. It occurs to me that if my watering automation project could go so haywire with horses, maybe there could be unexpected problems with humans, too.

I decide I should design extra cutoff switches to my robots and automated machine tool workstations as an added level of safety. My boss notices and thinks my ideas are excellent.

I'm basking in the aftermath of his praise when Nancy calls.

"We sold Charity!"

"What?"

"A man came by looking for thoroughbred broodmares for his brother-in-law in New Jersey. Charity has papers, and he bought her on the spot. The injuries to her face aren't important to them." I'm blown away. Talk about the perfect buyer. Maybe this horse rescuing business is okay. I decide to relax and quit worrying so much about things.

Shows how naïve I am.

**

The next day one of my automated work stations shorts out and I spend hours locating the problem and rewiring. I'm finally headed for my car when my boss corners me.

"Hey, Brad, I know it's short notice, but I need you to fill in for me and present a project proposal over at Crystal City tomorrow."

Crystal City is in Arlington, Virginia and home to the Naval Ship Systems Command. It's about thirty minutes away from the lab, but in the opposite direction from home.

Answering funding questions is not my favorite thing. It ranks

77

right below the thought of changing diapers and being near Junior. But there's no acceptable response I can give except yes. Getting approval and money for our projects is an important part of the job. And my boss has been steadily expanding my duties and opportunities. As bosses go, he's one of the truly good ones.

By the time I get home, I'm looking forward to dinner and a quiet night with Nancy. I'm informed otherwise when I arrive at our darkened house and find a note on the refrigerator.

"Gone to Charles Town with Sharon. Be back late."

Much better than "Gone Riding," but still disappointing. I should have noticed that the pickup and trailer were not parked in their usual spot in the driveway.

Charles Town is in West Virginia. That's about fifty miles away. Its claim to fame as far as Nancy and Sharon are concerned is that it's the proud location of two racetracks, Charles Town and Shenandoah Downs. The horses that run there are not the caliber of the ones at Churchill Downs in Kentucky or Santa Anita in California. In fact, horses that are too slow to win in West Virginia don't have many options left.

Their owners often tire of expensive training bills and are willing to sell them cheaply. One of the few other options for slow race horses is to end up at the same kind of auction that Skinny, Spyder, and Charity did.

It's less than twenty-four hours since Charity left and Nancy and Sharon are out looking to fill that empty stall already. Talk about money burning a hole in your pocket.

I'm hard at work, rehearsing tomorrow's presentation when Nancy calls.

"We're in Leesburg getting gas. We'll be home in twenty minutes."

"Did you --?" Silly question. Of course they did.

**

This time it's a five-year-old bay gelding. That's the same color as Junior, brown with a black mane and tail. He's thin, but not starving like the other rescues.

Four legs, a head, and a tail all in the right places. Perfectly normal.

He's so normal and so nice that in a matter of weeks he attracts a buyer. It's the teenage daughter of a Navy captain. She and her family come to ride the horse several times. They like him and they connect with us as we're a Navy family, too.

When the daughter and her mother arrive with a horse trailer and a veterinarian to check out the gelding, it's a happy, upbeat day with one exception. Nancy and Sharon are nervous because when they buy horses, they don't get to vet them.

Our vet gives them a once over, but not a full vetting as they can't be returned anyway.

He concentrates on getting them healthy. It's different for people who buy from us. The buyers' vets come and it's the first thorough vetting for soundness our rescue horses receive. Surprises are always possible.

I've also learned that what one vet passes, another may not.

Their vet spends an hour inspecting the horse. Nancy's relieved when he passes the gelding with flying colors. Since their family has decided against x-rays and their vet sees no need for any, the deal is consummated on the spot. The gelding gets his legs wrapped as a protection for the trip to his new home. Then he walks docilely into the new trailer. We wave goodbye to the family and the gelding.

**

Nancy and I are doing dinner dishes when we get the call. It's the Navy captain, father of the family that bought the gelding mere hours before. And he's yelling.

"Your horse is lame. We're bringing him back in the morning. We want all our money back." I look at Nancy, she shakes her head.

"The horse was sound when he left here. Your vet watched him load into your trailer."

The captain yells again, so I hold the phone away from my ear. Nancy tells me to ask what their vet says. I do. They haven't called him yet.

"I'm sorry something has happened, but I suggest you check with him and let us know what he says."

"I outrank you and I'm ordering you to take this horse back."

That's pretty scary for a Lieutenant Junior Grade to hear, and I can see the concern in Nancy's eyes.

"Let's see what your vet says."

"Take him back, or I'll report you for behavior unbecoming to a gentleman."

I still have a few weeks left in the service, and there's no way I want a negative mark on my record.

"Please call back tomorrow after the vet comes." The Captain is still threatening as I hang up the phone.

Nancy asks, "Can he do that?"

"I don't know."

"How could he get hurt in such a short time? It's terrible. He's such a sweet horse."

I know.

"Maybe we should give them their money back. But if it's a permanent injury, we can't sell him again. We'll lose all the money we invested in him."

No question she's right.

"But it's not worth your career. I think we should just take him back."

I can see the worry on her face. This threat to me has her really upset.

Needless to say, we don't sleep well.

**

It's hard for me to concentrate at work the next day. A bad mark on my Navy record will affect my entire life. I have a wife and soon a baby to care for. Visions of my future float through my mind. I keep opening my mouth to discuss the problem with my boss, also a Navy captain, but then I shut it again. What if he totally agrees with his counterpart? What if it changes his opinion of me?

I call home twice in the afternoon to see if the buyer contacted Nancy. But he hasn't.

After a long, nervous day, I'm mentally exhausted. It's dark out by the time I get home, and the vet must have seen the horse again. I make the decision to call the captain.

Their younger son answers the phone.

"Hello. May I speak with your father?"

"He's not home yet."

"Will you tell him that Brad Smith called? It's about the hurt horse."

"About when he fell out of the trailer? I saw him."

Whoa.

"What did you see?"

"He was on his knees. I fell on my knees last week, too. It hurts."

"I bet it does. Thanks. Please have your Dad call." I hang up the phone with a smile. As far as I'm concerned, we're not responsible.

Nancy heaves a sigh of relief when I tell her.

The captain's call later is short and civil. Their vet says the horse will be fine in a week. We agree that the horse belongs to his family. End of story.

Surprise, surprise, he doesn't mention the fall, nor does he apologize. I've never heard of a Navy captain behaving like that. I decide to give him the benefit of the doubt. Maybe he didn't know when he called yesterday.

That night I dream that I'm adrift in a rowboat. Out of the fog, the captain is bearing down on me with a battleship. I can't row fast enough to escape.

Maybe selling horses isn't as easy as I thought.

15

IT'S YOU AND ME AGAINST THE WORLD

The seasons change.

So do a lot of other things.

Sharon marries and we regrettably see less of her. We wish her the best, but I know how much Nancy misses her. Shortly after that, Sharon sells Bear to a new home.

As if to make up for Nancy's miserable first trimester, she has an easy delivery.

And suddenly we're the proud parents of a healthy, beautiful baby girl we name Lynn.

Nancy and I alternate on Lynn's night feedings. I love holding Lynn and watching her drink her bottle, but it's all a bit overwhelming. What about Lynn's future? Will I be a good Dad? Can I provide for her? Keep her safe and well?

Scary thoughts.

I finish the Dr. Spock baby books. Renee, our local Leesburg librarian, recommends more of the latest books on child rearing. To do anything well, I believe in preparation and education. I'm confident that the books can help me to be a perfect father, if I can just find the time to read them all.

Nancy has no interest in any of the books, which I hope will change. When I try to discuss the latest baby theories with her, she's not interested. Her regular response is, "All kids are different. I'll read when a problem comes up." She may not like reading about children, but she loves reading stories to Lynn. Fortunately, Lynn is a happy and healthy baby. And we promptly get pregnant again.

But something else changes. I notice that if we're out in the yard, Amy, the dog, stays near Lynn. And lately, if Nancy and Lynn are away, she'll actually hang out with me.

Nancy tells me that lots of dogs have trouble when a baby comes into the household. Her father had a Scottish Terrier named Funny that went to Yale with him.

He trained Funny to hide under the bed in the dorm room whenever the door opened.

He was as close to her father as Amy is to Nancy.

When Nancy's older sister was born, Funny passed away. Nancy remembers her mother saying the dog died of a broken heart, feeling left out. Amy has done the complete opposite. She's happily adopted Lynn.

I get a serious demonstration of this one Sunday afternoon. I'm enjoying the Sunday paper under the shade of the beech tree in our side yard. Next to me, Lynn happily plays with her inflated Roly-Poly penguin in her playpen. Amy sprawls nearby, sound asleep. Or so I think.

An unfamiliar car stops in front and a young man in a plaid shirt and jeans gets out.

From the corner of my eye, I notice Amy immediately tense and stand.

"Can I help you?" I ask the stranger as he approaches across the yard.

"I'm looking for the Smiths." As he gets closer, Amy moves in front of Lynn.

"I'm Brad Smith."

"Dennis. I heard you have a horse for sale. Is that right?"

"We do, but you'll need to talk with my wife. Unfortunately, she's out at the moment." We talk a bit longer and as Dennis leaves, he notices Lynn.

"What a sweet baby," he says. He moves toward her.

He tries to circle Amy to get a better look at the baby. I'm surprised to see Amy repeatedly insert herself between Dennis and Lynn. Nothing aggressive. No barking or growling. She just physically blocks his way. It's something she doesn't do when friends and family approach Lynn.

"What's wrong with your dog?" It takes me a minute to realize that Amy is deliberately preventing Dennis from getting close to the baby.

"I wouldn't go any closer. You'll upset the dog," I say.

Dennis backs away.

"Sorry. Didn't mean anything by it."

After he leaves, I look at Amy. She's already lying down against Lynn's playpen. Lynn reaches through a gap and pulls Amy's fur. Amy doesn't appear to mind at all.

For the first time I feel a real connection with Amy. We both have identical goals. Protecting Lynn.

I think I'll pop by the pet store tomorrow. Amy hasn't had a special treat in ages. Heck.

Maybe I'll buy her the whole darn store.

16

BUYING TROUBLE

Now we're a family of four - okay three and a half, I'm just rounding up. Nancy, Lynn, the baby on the way, and me. If I add Clarence, four horses and a dog, I guess we're really a family of ten. Yes, that's four horses. Three are Nancy's and Sharon's.

Luckily one isn't.

Seeing less riding time in the immediate future, Nancy rented our fourth stall to a friend of a friend's daughter, Izzy, for the summer. Izzy is a redhead with a perky dusting of freckles across her face. She takes her horse, a big gray thoroughbred gelding nicknamed Tony, to college with her during the school year, so he'll only be with us temporarily. The board money will help support Nancy's horses while we're dealing with our second pregnancy.

It pleases me that she's concerned with mitigating the cost of her horses. And with Izzy around, Nancy has a riding buddy.

My service in the Navy ends, but I continue to work for the Navy. That makes my pay slightly better. Good thing, because at the rate we're going, we'll need every penny. I plan to start job hunting for a better paycheck after the second baby arrives.

But first, we have a serious problem.

Our wonderful Great Falls house is no longer big enough. We need to move.

I want to find another rental in case I find a job opportunity elsewhere. Nancy wants to buy.

Sadly, we discover that we can't afford to buy or rent a bigger place in Great Falls. Many of the older farms are being divided up into large "Estates with Horses" properties. Estate is the polite word for mansion with land. Builders are suddenly grabbing up all the available property and bulldozing the old farm houses. Building has been booming in the last two years and so have prices. It's only a matter of time until our small rental house disappears too. Still, it shows what a good investment land can be.

By the time Nancy and I sit down to discuss our financial situation in relation to moving, I'm half convinced that buying a house is our best option. I may not be into animals, but making money is a different story.

"I'm willing to buy if you're willing to move if I get a good job offer elsewhere." There's a pause as she struggles with the idea.

"Agreed," She says finally. "That's fair." Nancy's idea of fairness is one of the things I love about her. She always tries to understand both sides of a problem.

"To find a house in our budget, we'll have to move further out." I continue.

"Okay."

"And it will have to be a fixer-upper"

"I can do the painting."

Oh, please no. "It probably won't be as nice as this house."

"It will be perfect."

Well, this is certainly going better than I expected. As long as I can keep her away from the paint.

"So what do you have in mind?" I ask.

"Ten to twenty acres, a livable house with three bedrooms, and a barn with a good roof that we can turn into stalls." Well, that's pretty specific. I guess she put some thought into this. Okay then.

We're in agreement. Even in the case of my having a future job location change, the possible future sale profit on owning a piece of land makes it worth the risk. If we can stay within our budget, we'll buy.

So the house hunting begins.

This will be the first real estate purchase for both of us. Since it's such a big investment, I make a serious effort to be smart about our approach. With some research, I pick an area east of Route 15 and north of Route 50 where it's still open land with old farms. It's between Fairfax and Aldie. The land is still inexpensive, but plans for extended freeway access in the area suggest property value could increase in years to come.

We make an appointment with Katherine Childs, a real estate agent who covers that area. She's tall, elegant, and, when she looks down through her gold framed glasses with their gold safety chain, a bit intimidating. I'm not surprised that no one has shortened her name to Kathy or Katy. This is not a woman for anything frivolous like a nickname.

"What do you have in mind?" she asks.

I give her our specifications and add, "Under thirty-eight-thousand dollars."

She nods. "Let's hop in my car. I have a few properties I can show you right now."

This is great. Sounds like Katherine's the right agent for us. I thought we might have a hard time finding something in our price range, but I guess not. I mention it to Katherine.

"Not to worry. This first property is a pinch higher than you mentioned, but I'm sure you'll see what a steal it is. Here we are." Her realty car turns off the road and up a driveway. A long, long driveway.

White, four-board fencing surrounds manicured fields on either side. Not a building in sight.

"I don't see the house," Nancy says.

"It's another half a mile. This property has the most gorgeous views. There's ice skating on the lake in the winter."

There's no lake in sight.

"The lake's over there beyond that hill."

I have to ask, "How big is this place?"

"Two-hundred-fifty acres."

"It's in our price range?"

"Of course not. That was totally unrealistic. There are no properties under fifty acres or under two thousand dollars an acre even for raw land. A small property with a house and a barn would be gobbled up long before it came on the market."

That's her idea of a "pinch" higher?

After a speedy trip back to the real estate office, Katherine barely says goodbye through her clenched teeth before she dumps us on the sidewalk.

"Bit testy, wouldn't you say?" I comment.

Nancy points out, "You may have crossed the line when you asked if the property had its own zip code."

**

We try another realty office and again explain our

specifications to the agent.

His laughter follows us out the door.

I have a characteristic Nancy doesn't know yet. When someone tells me no, it usually makes me dig in my feet and try harder. To my astonishment, she has the same response to negativity. We firmly believe there's a property somewhere that fits our description.

"People said the same thing when Sharon and I were hunting for a show horse with only two hundred dollars," she adds.

Unable to ride as she's in the latter stages of pregnancy, Nancy buckles Lynn into the pickup and drives around our selected area to look for farms while I'm at work.

At the end of three weeks, she finds two small properties. One is too expensive and the other is unlivable. But she refuses to be discouraged.

By week four, she pinpoints a small area, Aldie and Arcola, within the larger region we particularly like. It includes one of those charming, old fashioned, country stores that populate rural Virginia.

Usually owner or family-operated, they're small general stores with everything from food to hardware to ammunition. Mostly they have wood floors and barrels of pickles, just like I remember from childhood in Massachusetts. Those little stores from my past are long gone, so it's a treat to discover them dotted all over Virginia.

In addition to the normal goods, each is unique. One sells used furniture in the basement. At another, people line up in the summer months for the owner's scrumptious homemade peach ice cream. The owner of a third works as a neurosurgeon during the week, but loves the change of pace. His store has an old potbellied stove surrounded by benches. Each of these stores forms the center of all local gossip.

When I mention the local stores to Clarence, he says, "There's one that sells white lightning under the counter." I guess he would know. He tells us that as a young man, he used to run sugar for bootleggers down near the C&O Canal.

While at work one day, I get a call from Nancy. She's at a country store in Aldie and I can hear the excitement in her voice.

"Honey, I think I found it."

"A farm? Great. Tell me."

"I don't know any details yet. Can you meet me at Peterson's store after work? There'll still be a few hours of light."

Following directions, I arrive at Peterson's to find Nancy and Lynn waiting.

Nancy hurries me inside and introduces me to Ken Peterson. In his forties, he's of medium height and totally bald. Comfortable and congenial, he acts more like a host at a party than the owner of the store.

Apparently, Nancy has been dropping by for soft drinks and snacks while driving around the area. That's how she met Ken and his sister, Hailee, who also works at the store.

Hailee looks very similar to Ken, but thinner with long brown hair. Ken and Hailee hit it off with Nancy and the baby. They've taken an interest in our farm hunt.

I can see why Nancy likes them. They're kind, interesting people. After chatting a few moments, Ken steps to his phone and dials.

"What's going on," I ask Nancy.

"He's calling the owners to see if they're home so we can stop by." Before I can ask anything else, Ken turns and gives us the thumbs up sign.

Moments later, we're driving down a wooded dirt road.

"How did you ever manage to find this place?"

"See all those sold signs?" We had passed several parcels of partially wooded, partially open land with sold signs.

"There's one piece right in the center with a house and a big barn and no for sale sign. I couldn't tell if it was for sale or sold or what. Nobody was home. So I came down to the store to call the number on the signs to see what I could find out. I mentioned it to Ken. Turns out he knows the owners. They're an older couple who divided up their large farm and sold off parts of it, but they kept the house, barn, and eighteen acres until they're ready to retire in Florida. Ken thinks they're ready to put it on the market."

"Does he know how much?"

She shakes her head. "Here we are."

We turn down a sloping driveway and through a big stand of oak trees. I see a big, old red barn on the left and a small, old, white-washed house beyond it at the bottom of the slope. It looks perfect. Could this be it? My excitement rises.

We meet the owners at the gate to the house yard. They invite us inside for coffee and cookies. They're Martha and Bill, in their mid to late seventies. She's tiny and a pistol. He's a tall, frail, and thin as a flagpole.

Martha's eyes light up when she spots Lynn in my arms. She insists on holding her. Thank goodness there's no resistance from Lynn as she good-naturedly meets another new person.

As we enter, we discover the house is actually a log cabin. On the outside, there's a narrow, glassed-in porch across the front. It hides the construction of the cabin section of the house. How old is this place?

I notice the floor tilts markedly toward one corner. Bill answers my unasked questions.

"Over 250 years old," Bill says. "This section is a pre-revolutionary slave cabin. Cabins don't have any foundations, so the corner that the sun defrosts first in the spring settles more. The 'new' wing with the living room and two small rooms above it were added in 1916. All the land in this area was originally part of a royal grant to Lord Fairfax."

"We've come about the property," I start.

Martha cuts me off. "Tell us about yourselves and this beautiful baby."

We do, feeling a little awkward, but the conversation is pleasant. We like Martha and Bill immediately. Finally, I get to turn the tables and ask about them.

Martha jumps in first. "I worked in a condom factory except during WWII. Then I was a flight trainer for pilots."

"Like Pancho Barnes, the woman aviator?" Nancy asks.

"Exactly. There were a bunch of us back then."

"Were you a pilot, too?" I ask Bill.

"Heck, no," comes from Martha. "I tried to teach him and he nearly killed us when he froze on the stick while we were landing. I couldn't get control of the plane."

"What'd you do?"

"I knocked him out with a wrench and landed the plane." She laughs.

Nancy and I are aghast.

"Only thing I could do or we both would have died."

Bill shrugs. "I'm an accountant."

Martha continues, "We have a licensed airfield right here on the farm. A grass one. It runs down the field beside the house. You can't see it now because the grass has grown up, but it's there."

"It's been sold already," Bill adds.

I recognize the perfect opening and plunge in.

"We heard this property might be for sale?"

"We're planning on putting it on the market in another month and then heading south." Bill speaks up. "There's eighteen acres with the house and barn and all those wonderful old oak trees."

"We're particularly anxious about those trees," Martha cuts in. "We have people drive in all the time and want to buy them for lumber. And if a builder buys the property, we're afraid he'll level the place and sell off all the trees."

"Are those the trees in the front? They're beautiful. Who could ever cut them down?" Nancy says.

I nod in agreement. Some of the oaks we saw were over three feet in diameter.

Bill and Martha smile at each other. They like our reaction.

Three weeks later, a real estate lawyer draws up the purchase papers for a price less than our budget. As we finish, he makes an odd remark.

"I expect I'll see you again soon."

"I'm sure we'll see you around," I respond.

"No, I meant professionally. I bet you won't be able to hold on to this property."

"I assure you we can afford-"

"-No, no. I mean you'll be getting so many offers that you'll be selling it soon."

Nancy and I laugh politely.

"You'll see," he says as we leave.

Our children are going to grow up in a log cabin. I wonder if either or both will become president.

17

LOVE, HONOR, AND MUCK

Moving to our new farm goes smoothly with one exception. The old red barn housed cattle for years. What we took for a dirt floor is over a foot of packed and dried cow poop. Thank goodness the smell is all dried up, too. It takes weeks of backbreaking work to dig it all out.

I don't remember promising to "Love, honor, and muck barns."

In addition, there's no water or electricity at the barn. My electrical engineering expertise has some benefits. I hire a ditch digging machine for one day to run a trench from the barn to the log cabin. I'll insert water pipes and a power cable in the trench and cover it over on my next day off. Piece of cake, I think.

And then it rains. The ditch fills with water, caving in on the sides. All the removed dirt washes back into the ditch. Before I can get the time to hand-shovel it out, there's a hard freeze. But working in the warmer afternoons, I manage to shovel half of the ditch clear. Then it rains again. That piece of cake job is definitely sour lemon.

I change plans. Before I clear the trench again, I lay out the water pipes and power cable beside the trench. This time, as I clear it out, I push the pipe and cable in immediately. My back is killing me by the time I'm done. I'll need a backrub when I get back to Great Falls.

**

Our farm is a long rectangle of land with an entrance on one of the short ends.

The gravel driveway stays close to the left side, passing the barn about a quarter of the way down, and ending at the house a little farther on. In front of the house lies an ugly pile of bulldozed sheds. Martha told us that there's a little building the size of a phone booth underneath. She claims it was formerly the smallest liquor store in Virginia.

There is no way we can confirm it, and we have no idea why it's here on this property.

Martha doesn't explain that part. The huge oak trees cover the front right corner and continue down the long right side of the driveway.

As we're preparing to move in, Nancy worries that the fencing in the back woods may have gaps where the horses can get out. I figure if any horse can, it will be Junior. Especially if there's any water on the other side. Nancy sends me out to check it.

Amy walks the entire boundary with me as I inspect the fences for gaps. I repair a couple of broken spots. The wild vines are thick in several places, but they're so dry in the winter that it's easy to break them off. Otherwise, the wire fencing is in decent condition.

I take a deep breath and look around. It's a beautiful winter day, crisp and sunny. I find myself whistling. It's even a pleasure to have Amy with me. As we near the house, I reach down and pet her. This is the first property I've ever owned. It feels good, even if it is a farm.

I head back in the house to help with the unpacking. Tonight will be our first night sleeping in the log cabin.

I join Nancy and help putting away dishes in the kitchen. Lynn's sleeping, happily ensconced in the small second floor bedroom. The other small bedroom waits, ready for the new baby.

Their rooms are on the second floor of the "new" 1916 wing of the log cabin, which has level floors. Clarence has settled into the enclosed porch. He has level floors.

Our bedroom over the kitchen in the log cabin doesn't-and we didn't realize how steep that slope was.

For the move, we used the pickup, the horse trailer and the help of several friends. Nancy and I have worked all day in the downstairs part of the house.

Finally it's time for bed. Lynn's asleep, and we're alone. I pick up Nancy and head up the stairs. I hadn't carried her over the threshold of the Great Falls house, so it feels appropriate now. I know our friends set up our bedroom in the afternoon, but I haven't been upstairs since then.

Nancy's a little heavier than I remember. Uh, oh. I forgot about the coming baby. That's another thirty pounds. I manage to reach the top of the stairs. Nancy laughs at me. Afraid to pause and reach for a light, I stagger to where I think the bed is.

When I bump into it, I place her on the bed. Well, not exactly "place." The last few inches are more of a drop.

Nancy shrieks.

Alarmed, I reach for the light and switch it on.

There's Nancy, flipped sideways against the wall on the far

side of the bed.

When I put - okay, dropped her - on the bed, I wasn't thinking about the angle of the floor.

She's rolled all the way across it. Luckily the bed was against the wall to stop her.

Thank goodness, she thinks it's funny. Her giggles make me laugh too. We certainly won't forget our first night in the log cabin. But I'm definitely cutting blocks to level up the bed first thing tomorrow.

The next day, we're unpacking books in the living room when a neighbor from a mile down the road stops by to introduce himself. His overalls and wool shirt tell us he's a serious farmer. He's in his thirties, and has a pink, sunburned face and dark curly hair. For some reason, he seems very uncomfortable talking with us.

"I'm Curtis. My mom said to tell you welcome. If'n you ever need some mowing or help, you just stop by the house and let us know. Got my own tractor and bush hog."

All the time he talks, Curtis holds his cap in his hands and stares at the floor.

He'll glance up occasionally at me, but never looks at Nancy. Surely he's seen a pregnant woman before?

"Lovely to meet you, Curtis." Nancy says.

Still no eye contact with her.

"Ma'am."

"Thanks for stopping by. We'll definitely need some help." I walk him out to his old Chevy pickup.

"Almost forgot. Mom sent a welcome present." Curtis reaches in the bed of his truck and removes a Xerox size box.

"Can't have a farm without one of these." He thrusts the box into my hands and drives off.

Something moves inside the box. I almost drop it. Instead, I quickly lower it to the ground.

"What's that?" Nancy asks. She peeks inside and closes the lid back quickly.

"What is it?" I ask.

"Just a present for the barn."

"What?"

"I'll run it on up there." Before she can leave, I reach over and lift the top.

"That's a black cat."

Nancy pushes the lid down.

"No, it's a black and white cat. White chest and at least two feet."

"I don't care what color it is. No cats. Put the box in the car. I'll take it back."

"That would be rude. Besides, it's a great gift. We'll need a cat in the barn to keep the mice down. Might as well be this one."

I hate her logic. I guess it can live in the barn. I won't be going there much.

18

WHAT'S NEW PUSSYCAT?

Unpacking turns out to be more arduous than I expected. With Nancy only a short time away from delivering our second child, she shouldn't lift anything. But every time I turn my back, she tries to help. Lynn is almost one year old and getting around on her own, so we need to watch her constantly.

I'm definitely feeling sad about leaving Great Falls. Who knew our life there would be so good. And although they complained that we lived too far away from the city, our friends managed to visit frequently.

My old college roommate and his wife even came out in a snowstorm to stay with us for Christmas. The roads got so bad, they were forced to abandon their car when they hit a snow drift and hike the last mile to our house.

The storm ended overnight. After a slow morning of opening presents and a late breakfast, I noticed the snow plows had gone by. I drove my roommate to pick up his car and bring it to the house. But we couldn't find it.

"Are you sure this is the spot?" I ask.

"Yeah, I remember we walked past that yellow mailbox."

"So where is it?" We drive all the way to the turn off from Route 193.

No car.

A quick drive back to the house and ten phone calls later we dial a garage in Great Falls.

"Yeah, the car with the bullet holes. We towed it in last night late," the mechanic says.

"Right, the one with the bullet holes," my friend says, then mouths to me, "This guy's a real joker."

We head straight to the garage. As we approach the office, we notice his car parked on the side.

He stares a moment and then hurries over. I follow quickly and I'm amazed when I get closer. Bullet holes actually do riddle the driver's side of the vehicle.

We're stunned.

When we question the tow driver, he has no answers. A deputy called him to come pick it up. It was blocking the plow.

We call the Sheriff's office. They have no information either. They did notice the bullet holes.

"...thirty-eight caliber bullets," the deputy tells us. Six of them. Someone emptied their entire pistol.

Who killed my friend's car? We'll probably never know, but I can just imagine the conversation between my friend and his insurance agent.

Probably something like "Tell me again what happened to your car?"

On the good side, it didn't deter him and his wife from visiting afterwards. Nor did it stop any of our other friends from visiting, but I'm not so sure if they will continue to come as far as our new place. I'll certainly be disappointed if they don't.

Moving brings all sorts of changes. Who knows what kind of life we'll have at this new farm?

Nancy and I are carrying a pile of empty boxes out to the pick-up, when a large orange cat comes out of nowhere and zips right into the log cabin's open front door. It's so fast, I'm not sure I've even seen it, but I can tell by Nancy's face that she spotted it, too. She heads after it in quick pursuit.

I'm adamant about not allowing cats in the house. I won't have one scratching Lynn or the new baby the way I was as a child.

By the time I get inside, Nancy has the cat cornered on the sink. She waves me back as she tries to move close enough to grab it. She slips forward and reaches out.

The cat makes a heroic leap to the table and a second jump to the linoleum floor.

Legs scrambling, it disappears into the living room.

"Wait here," I tell Nancy. "I'll get it." I should have saved my breath. Nancy gets there ahead of me.

The cat dives under the sofa at what must be an indoor speed record. Nancy kneels, but her arms aren't long enough to reach.

"Get a spoon of Amy's dog food." I'm back in seconds with the food. Nancy waves it under the sofa in front of the cat.

"Come and get it," she croons.

After five more minutes of "here kitty, kitty," it's obvious the food isn't working.

"Let me try," I hear myself saying. "My arms are longer." She pushes back so I can take her place. I reach gingerly under the sofa.

The cat's in the back corner near the wall. If I really reach, I can just touch its tail. I stretch. I can feel its fur- MEROW! The terrified cat shrieks and makes tracks out from under the sofa.

105

Unfortunately the route it chooses is straight up my inner arms using all its claws for traction.

The cat flees through the kitchen at top speed, spots the open front door, and hastily escapes.

I, on the other hand, am still in the living room writhing on the floor.

It's Nurse Nancy to the rescue. She carefully cleans what I'm sure will be my permanently scarred arms. She stops the bleeding and applies ointment.

I end up looking like Frankenstein's monster with Band-Aids plastered up and down both arms. I can already hear my office mates snickering when I arrive at work tomorrow.

I don't care. I'm feeling very sorry for myself.

Nancy gives me a look. "This wouldn't have happened if you hadn't scared the cat."

Me? No way it's my fault? I rail against cats. I hate cats. I never want to see another cat. Nancy totally ignores me.

When I finally wind down, she kisses my forehead.

"Are you done?"

I nod.

19

NANCY GETS THE BLUES

It's a month past when our second child is due. December 31st. New Year's Eve and a big blizzard is forecast.

Of course, that's when Nancy's water breaks. An hour later, and with hurried calls to assorted family, friends, and the doctor, we arrive at the hospital. No sooner do we get there than the expected blizzard starts. Thank goodness Nancy didn't go into labor a couple of hours later. We are definitely at the right place to be snowed in under the circumstances.

Lynn is with Nancy's mother, a short distance from the hospital. Clarence is in charge of the farm and animals. Luckily he doesn't have to lead any horses in and out. On the new farm, he only has to open doors. All bases covered.

In the late afternoon, Nancy delivers our second child. Mom and baby are healthy. Nancy and I grin ear-to-ear. The baby grins too, but I suspect it's gas. Now we have two beautiful daughters. We name the baby Anne, a favorite name of Nancy's.

We even qualify for the tax break.

**

Once we get the entire family settled in at home, I uncover a serious problem.

Not the kids. They're happy and no trouble. Anne is soon sleeping all the way through the night. I think she's going to be a sweet, contented baby, too.

It's Nancy who's miserable. I can tell how much she loves our daughters, but when she isn't with them I notice her smile fades.

I ask if she can tell me what's wrong.

"It feels as if my riding has come to a sudden stop and will never start again. Why do I have to give up one joy for the other?"

It was a fair question. I hadn't realized, but I should have.

We were fine in Great Falls with Lynn, but now that we moved to Aldie, we don't know anyone nearby. I hadn't thought about the fact that we are sitting on Nancy's dream farm, yet she can't leave the children alone to even go for a ride. Wow.

No wonder she's miserable. I think I'd go nuts too if I couldn't do the work I love.

Not to mention that we have seven horses in the barn eating their heads off and not being exercised. We're up to seven because I keep forgetting Nancy abhors a vacuum. I need to get that tattooed on my forehead. What was I thinking when we bought an eighteen-acre farm? The last months of pregnancy may have slowed Nancy down in the riding department, but she used that time to find a few more needy horses.

The problem is simple. Unfortunately the solution isn't. We need some help so Nancy can spend a couple of hours a day in the barn while the kids are napping. But even if we can find some help, we have no money to pay them. Every penny of my salary is budgeted tightly.

I worry as this unhappy state of affairs continues until May with Nancy only able to ride on the weekends when I'm home. Then I have a brainstorm. The solution is right in front of us. We have no money, but we have horses. Lots of horses. Who baby-sits? Young girls. What do young girls like? Horses.

I suggest we put an ad in the newspaper: "Will trade riding lessons for babysitting and barn work."

Nancy thinks my idea is brilliant.

It's amazing. Thirty nice preteens and teenagers respond.

After holding extensive interviews with the kids and their parents, we pick two people instead of one. They're fifteen-year-old twin sisters, Taylor and Dana. The girls are great. Warm, friendly, and truly nice. Their mother, a lovely woman who works two jobs to support her family is delighted. Taylor will work with Nancy in the barn and Dana prefers babysitting Lynn and Anne.

Nancy's smile tells me how well my idea is working out. I love seeing that smile as her energy returns. It's nice to be the hero for a change. I'm so busy basking in her praise and some much desired thank you kisses, that I almost miss it when she says, "I know right where we can get the perfect pony for Taylor and Dana."

"Whoa? What? Another horse? Wait, that wasn't part of my idea."

"But, honey," She explains, "The Taylor and Dana need a quiet, experienced horse, not a spooky, jumpy one like those we buy on the racetrack to retrain and sell. Riding is dangerous, especially when you're learning. It's important that they're safe. We need a horse that's bombproof."

"Surely people don't throw bombs at horses?" I blurt out. Immediately there's that look. The one that says, "Knock it off." I can't argue after I think about it. She's right. Safety first. So much for my brainstorm to save money.

She heads to the phone and, faster than Riva Ridge won the Kentucky Derby, we acquire a new pony. I hate to think what Nancy could arrange given more time.

"Perfect," Nancy informs me as she hangs up the phone. "My friend has a large Connemara pony that her kids have outgrown and it needs a good home. Don't worry, he didn't cost a penny."

Yeah, well, I'm a seasoned horse "acquirer" now. I know there's no such thing as a free horse. I'm fairly sure the new pony plans to eat. Then he'll want new shoes once a month, blankets to keep him warm, and all the rest of it.

Before I can object, Nancy's lips meet mine. "Thank you," she whispers, "for the brilliant idea." Oh, what the heck. Some people are driven to bankruptcy. Our family will arrive on horseback.

A week later, as I mow the yard, an unfamiliar station wagon with a Hartman horse trailer rolls down our driveway.

Horse, or pony in this case, number eight has arrived.

Of course I have to ask. "What's the difference between a horse and a pony?" I'm told a pony is fourteen hands two inches or less from the ground to the withers at the top of the shoulder. A hand equals four inches. So a pony is basically a short horse.

Taylor informs me that I'm only partially right. Some breeds of horses are always small. Like Shetland ponies.

Great. The twins already know more about horses and ponies than I do.

Nancy watches while holding Lynn and Anne. Taylor and Dana stand by in breathless anticipation as the trailer parks. The driver is a tall, elderly man, dressed in a yellow vest and plaid wool shirt over faded corduroys. He politely tips his hat to the ladies and then to me. I shake his hand in welcome.

"I'm Ed," he tells us.

Taylor can't wait any longer. "What's his name?"

"Figgy," Ed responds. "You'll find he's an unusual pony."

"Unusual" sounds like an odd description for a pony. I'm about to ask when he backs a large white pony with a mild demeanor out of the trailer.

I notice the happy faces of the girls. Taylor and Dana ooh and ah. Nancy holds Lynn and Anne up to pat Figgy. Lynn is now eighteen months and Anne five months.

They both are completely comfortable around the animals. I know they didn't get that from me.

Taylor steps forward and takes proprietary control of the lead shank. Dana strokes his neck. The costs in my head disappear. This much pleasure is priceless.

Figgy stands quietly as the kids touch him, showing no alarm at the strange surroundings and new people.

Nancy is clearly delighted. She catches my eye and smiles. I love that smile. I grin goofily in response. The sun comes out, the earth shakes, and angels sing Hosannas. I turn into a blithering idiot as always.

If I'd been smart, I would have paid more attention to the angels' choice of music. It wasn't my favorite, "Can't Take My Eyes Off Of You." It was Figgy's own personal theme song, "Don't Fence Me In."

20

TO BEEF OR NOT TO BEEF

It's tax time. Ever since I collected the year's receipts and statements on the barn, I catch tense glances from Nancy when she thinks I'm not looking. I wonder why until I add the numbers. She's definitely worried there won't be enough money for our kids and the horses.

Nancy offers to help with the taxes, but, like cooking and cleaning, I know math isn't her strong suit. I've had to straighten out her checkbook numerous times already, followed by swift dashes to the bank with deposits to prevent her checks from bouncing. Most of the time, I get to the bank fast enough.

It's her big, blue eyes I'd married her for, not her math ability, so I'm not complaining.

Out of curiosity, I decide to add up our food bills. The total is way worse than I expected. Feeding the four of us, plus the twins when they're here, and occasionally Clarence, isn't cheap. I've noticed that peanut butter rules at lunch time. I've seen Dana make peanut butter sandwiches. She adds ketchup, and then squashes them flat before biting into them. Don't ask. Nancy's not

113

much better. She crumples potato chips and spreads them over her peanut butter. Taylor and I are straight PB and J people.

Macaroni and cheese, burgers, and hotdogs are our quick and cheap dinner staples. Some chicken here and there. Nancy's still trying to learn to cook. So no one is exactly eating high on the hog. Hmmmm. High on the hog...

Here we are living on a farm, and we aren't raising any food. Eighteen acres and not a pig or a cow or a chicken. No garden. No fruit trees. Nothing. Nada. Between the horses and the people, we have a lot of mouths that ingest food, but nothing that makes food.

By the time I finish the taxes, I have a plan to lower those food bills and provide fresh and healthy food for everyone. We are going to grow our own.

As we climb into bed, I broach the subject with Nancy.

"What do you think about having a cow, some chickens, and a garden? We can save a lot of money." She shakes her head. "Between the horses, the house, the barn, the cooking, and two babies, I can't handle what I'm doing now. Besides, the cats and dogs will make short shrift of any chickens. As for a cow, there's no way I can care for one and then send it off to slaughter and eat it when it comes back."

"If I remember right, I saw you eat a hamburger tonight."

"It wasn't a cow I knew personally."

"I want a cow. You have seven horses and a pony. I can have one cow."

"Don't expect me to eat it." She rolls so her back faces me, and pulls the covers over her head.

I've learned the hard way that this move means the conversation is over. Well, it might be the end to our conversation, but I'm not going to back down on this.

We rarely ever disagree, but when we do, water usually ends the argument. The water fights originally started back in Great Falls. We must have been in the bathroom or kitchen, because one of us will flick water at the other if we disagree about something. The other flicks water back and then it escalates.

If Nancy sees me filling a cup with water while we're arguing, she'll run. Since we don't want thrown water in the house, she races for an outside door. By the time my cup is full and I pursue her, she's waiting for me in the yard armed with the garden hose. Pretty quickly, we're soaked and laughing. Argument over.

I'm not sure what our close neighbors in Great Falls, the landlord's brother, Ted, and his wife, thought of our water battles. They were frequently out on their porch as Nancy and I would go racing by with some form of water container or other in our hands.

The water fights have continued here. And now we can even refill from the kids' plastic wading pool.

Of course, if the water doesn't work to end an argument, the classic maneuver of taking all your clothes off usually does. The only serious fight we've ever had was over which route to take to visit a friend. That battle escalated because we were driving in the car and neither water nor removing clothes was a practical way to end it without getting arrested.

But this time is different. This is serious. I know I'm right. The very word farm means agriculture to me. We live on a farm. Logic says we should grow food.

What Nancy says about Amy and the black barn cat making short shrift of chickens makes sense. We expect the cat to hunt for meat and keep the mouse population down. Chickens would be an enticing gourmet menu item.

115

Chickens who spend their lives surrounded by predators probably wouldn't be relaxed enough to lay eggs even if they survived. So chickens are out.

But there's no reason why we can't have a garden. I imagine rows of corn, tomatoes, bell peppers, and potatoes. Maybe some carrots, radishes, and lettuce. Two acres sounds about right for a good, self-sustaining garden. Of course, I'll need a tractor and a plow.

And a cow. We have plenty of grass. The dogs and cats won't bother a cow. It will fit right in with all those horses. Our meat will be antibiotic and chemical free. Much healthier for all of us.

I fall asleep counting cows jumping over a fence. The cows wear tomatoes and lettuce impaled on their horns like shish-kabobs and garlands of ripe, golden corn around their necks.

**

The subject doesn't resurface, but Nancy and I share a chilly breakfast. I have to admit, I'm annoyed by her lack of support. Why can't she appreciate my plan this time?

She raved about my idea of trading lessons for help.

I think about it all week. I even borrow some books on gardening and raising beef from the library. Renee, the sweet, seventy-year-old librarian in Leesburg is very supportive. She directs me to the appropriate sections.

I fill my lunch hours at work researching which types of vegetables grow best in our area and which breeds of cow produce the best meat. I decide to start with the cow first.

When I'm ready, I head to see Ken down at the store. He's better than the yellow pages for finding information. He'll know where to buy a cow.

I arrive at Ken's store on my way home from work.

Unfortunately, everyone else has stopped by on their way home as well, and the place is packed. I recognize a few familiar faces and exchange greetings as I wait for Ken to have a few minutes free.

I look around as the crowd slowly dissipates. I never knew there's such a thing as bubble gum flavored chewing tobacco. Or a chocolate-flavored soft drink named Yahoo. The store has pickles, pickled beets, pickled hard boiled eggs, and pickled pigs' feet. If it's pickled, it's here. In the back is a weigh station for game. Hunting and fishing licenses are sold at the cash register. You can buy gas and oil for your car and oil for cooking. It's great one stop shopping.

Finally, it's my turn at the counter. I glance around. The only customers remaining besides me are the Edmonds, father and son. You would know they were related even without their matching beards and overalls. They have the same ruddy, suntanned faces, brown eyes, broad shoulders, and deep voices.

I don't know them, but I've heard they have a big corn operation over toward Leesburg. Their backs are turned as they check out ammunition.

I plunk a Yahoo on the counter. I have to try one.

"That it for you, Brad?" Ken asks in his Southern drawl. "Nancy and the girls were in this afternoon. Lynn and Anne are growing fast."

"They sure are. Have you got a minute to talk? I want to buy a cow."

There are chuckles behind me from the Edmonds.

Edmond, the younger, says, "Steer."

I don't understand.

"You want a steer, not a cow. 'Less you plannin' on milkin' it," he adds.

I get it and nod my thanks. But I can still hear their amused chuckles behind me.

Edmond, the elder, whispers to his son, "He works for the gov'ment. You can't 'spect too much."

That's my goal in life. Adding humor to people's lives.

I rephrase the question to Ken. "I'm looking for a steer."

Edmond, the elder, gives me an encouraging thumbs up as I continue.

"An Angus or maybe an angus mix." I quote from my research.

Again approving nods from the Edmonds. My research has paid off.

"What would a young steer cost, and who, around here, might have one for sale?"

Ken thinks a minute. "Angus are expensive. You sure that's what you want?"

Encouraged by the Edmonds, I nod. "Or a mix."

"Then you're looking at about four to five hundred dollars."

Whoa. That was more than double what I had budgeted.

Ken reads the disappointment on my face.

"Maybe something other than an Angus?" I shake my head.

I thank Ken and the Edmonds and head home. The Yahoo soft drink is pretty good, but the fun has gone out of my day. I mull over the math after dinner.

A steer weighs X amount of pounds at purchase. If the steer doubles or triples its weight and I divide the costs of feeding, vet bills, and the purchase price I could end up saving a nice amount for all the work. Yet there's also the risk of losing it to some unknown disease, or a broken leg. Then the net gain would be minus five hundred dollars. Way too high a risk on my salary. I guess I'll have to be content with a big garden.

Still, we do have to cut back the budget. I sit Nancy down for a serious talk about money.

"There's no way we can afford to keep eight horses," I open. "Is there any way we can cut down to say four, including Figgy for the twins.

"I'm working on a plan so the rescues don't cost us anything." This is news.

She reads the doubt on my face.

"What I'm thinking is that we keep track of the expenses of the horses we rescue and retrain and then sell them for an amount that covers their costs. Then we'd only pay for the horses we keep, like Junior and Figgy. What we really need are more horses with a bigger turnover to help pay for the expenses of the horses we just give away. Then I can stay home with the kids and we can still rescue needy horses."

Not at all what I had in mind. But her plan actually makes sense. I need to think about it. Any additional money would certainly help. If Nancy gets an off-the-farm job, any income would be eaten up by day care for the kids. We can't ask the twins to take on that kind of full time responsibility.

Next morning at breakfast I admit, "I agree it might work. Let's keep a set of books to watch how the cash flow goes. After six months if it's not working, you'll agree to cut down to four horses." Down to four horses? Did those words actually come out of my mouth?

"Deal?"

"Deal."

21

DON'T FENCE ME IN

Taylor and Dana turn out to be wonderful. Taylor's outgoing and wants to learn all about the horses. Dana's quieter and prefers being with the kids and the dogs and cats with the exception of Figgy. She and Figgy already have a special bond. Both girls impress us with their common sense. And most importantly, Lynn and Anne connect with them immediately.

When school ends, the twins stay over most days with us. Their older brother drives them back and forth and staying over saves him trips.

The twins and Izzy, if she's visiting, play Monopoly, card games, and croquet in the backyard. They also color and enjoy games with Lynn and Anne. In fact, they get so involved that it isn't long before they even show up with their own water pistols to join in our water fights.

Being around the twins feels very natural and their presence helps me become a better parent. Much more so than all the books I read on child raising.

Taylor and Dana have very clear opinions about almost

everything and, as they get more comfortable with us, seem to have no trouble expressing their points of view.

Nancy insists I listen carefully to what the young ones have to say and take them seriously. In doing so, I'm finding that they make surprisingly interesting points.

Having the twins, plus Lynn and Anne around, makes it hard to worry about every little thing the kids do. I find I'm actually relaxing a bit about being a parent.

One day, I'm headed down to Peterson's and ask the girls if they'd like me to bring them anything.

"Yahoos," Taylor says and Dana echoes.

I have to laugh. Ken's converted two more customers.

It's amazing how quickly our lives return to a good balance because of the twins' presence. I love seeing Nancy smile all the time again.

Figgy, however, may not be such a prize.

Since it's late June, the nights are warm and bugs are out during the day. The summer schedule means the horses are turned out at night and stay in their stalls during the heat of the day. This morning, when Nancy goes to bring the horses in for their breakfast, Figgy is already in his stall waiting. She looks to Clarence. He shrugs.

Nancy closes the door on Figgy's stall. After she brings all the other horses in, she sends me out to walk the fence.

I protest. "The fences are fine. I already walked all around, and there are no holes."

"Then why is he in the barn?"

"Teleportation?"

She doesn't appreciate my humor. Five minutes later, I'm walking the fences.

"There isn't a hole anywhere." I report an hour later.

Nancy accepts my findings, but I can tell she's worried.

"We've already discovered he can open and close all the stall doors. I've had to add special catches to keep him from doing it."

"Maybe a gate wasn't closed all the way?" I offer.

"No, everything was okay when I brought the rest of the horses in. If I don't know how he got out, he can do it again, either by himself or with others. He could get hurt. Thank goodness we shut the driveway gate last night." I don't know what to say.

The next morning, Figgy's waiting in the barn again. Nancy's beside herself.

Fortunately, the grain for the horses is in a closed room and unreachable. If he got into that and ate too much, he could be seriously ill. Like a kid eating too much candy.

"Honey, why don't we get up before dawn tomorrow? If he's still in the field, try to spot how he's getting out." It's the only thing I can think of.

Before dawn, we creep out of the back kitchen door and crouch where we can see the horses. I can make them out in the dim light, quietly grazing near the front of the field. Figgy's white coat is the easiest to see. He's still where he should be.

Twenty minutes later, it's considerably lighter out. Taylor slips out of the back door and quietly joins us. Dana watches from the window with Lynn and Anne.

Moments later, Figgy's head comes up. Nancy squeezes my hand. He walks directly toward the gate, takes two trotting steps and pops over it with ease. Then he casually walks up the hill to the barn and disappears inside.

Nancy gasps. "That gate is four and a half feet high."

"Is that big?"

"Huge. And he could have jumped the fence instead which is a little lower, but he didn't bother."

Two hours later, Nancy's on the phone with the lady who gave us Figgy. She's smiling when she hangs up.

"Turns out Figgy is a bit of an escape artist. Ed was supposed to warn us when he dropped him off. It started when their son was young. They have a neighbor who bakes a lot of cookies for her church meetings. The neighbor would meet my friend's son at her back door as he rode by with his friends and give them all cookies. Her son shared his with Figgy. He learned to like cookies.

Later, Figgy would smell the fresh baked cookies in the afternoon. He would pop over my friend's four-board wooden fence, head down their dirt road, and end up at the neighbor's back door. She would feed him a cookie. About that time, the school bus would pass. Figgy would race it home and jump back into his appropriate field just as her son got off the bus. After that, Figgy just kind of goes where he wants," the friend admitted.

"But they live way back from any traveled roads," I point out. "We're only a third of a mile from the hardtop road in one direction and a couple of miles from the highway in the other."

"I know. It might be a problem. I'd hate to send him back."

"No, please don't send him back."

We'd forgotten that the twins could hear us from the next room. They look very anxious as they hover in the doorway.

Nancy tries to alleviate their worries. "Let's just wait and see how it works out. You can help. We need to be sure the driveway gate and the barn doors are closed every night."

"We can do that," Taylor blurts out.

"Then we should be fine. Who's riding first today?"

"Me," comes from Dana.

That surprises me. It sounds as if Dana's overcoming her timidity with the horses.

That afternoon, as I plant the corn in our newly plowed garden, I have to laugh. I'd asked Nancy to call Curtis and arrange for him to come do the plowing. Curtis mumbled so badly on the phone Nancy couldn't understand a word he said. She finally told him I would phone. I did and had no trouble working out the details for the job.

Right before I hung up, Curtis asked, "You'll be there when I arrive, won't you?"

"If I'm not, Nancy will be here all day."

"Okay." But he doesn't sound too enthusiastic. I wonder what that's about.

I pause for a moment and look around. Up in the ring in the front paddock Dana trots into sight on Figgy with Nancy supervising. Down at the house, Taylor has the kids out in the yard playing.

A sky blue Cadillac rolls down the driveway. The car stops near Nancy and a middle-aged woman sticks her head out. She and Nancy talk for a second and then the Cadillac backs up the driveway and leaves. Probably another one of the pesky real estate agent trying to buy our farm. Our lawyer's warning was right on the money. Agents roll in here constantly. We should put a sign up, No Real Estate Agents Welcome.

Amy wanders up towards me to check out what I'm doing. When she nears me, I notice she has a stick in her mouth. I call her to me and take the stick. I've seen Nancy and the kids throw the stick for Amy to chase, but I have never tried it myself.

Amy goes on alert as I raise the stick. Her energy is amazing. I throw as hard as I can, yet she's where it's going to land a split second before it does. Amazing. When she brings it back, I heave it again as far as I can. She's still there first. Next time, I try to trick her about the direction I'm going to throw. She's beats the stick again.

I realize I'm smiling ear-to-ear. The complicated project I'm completing at work has disappeared from my mind. So has my list of farm jobs for the weekend. I'm in the moment and everything feels great with the world. Does everyone with a dog have this much fun?

22

GHOSTS AND ROBBERS

A few weeks later, I arrive home after dark. The gate across the driveway near the barn is closed, so I get out to open it.

The twins rush out of the barn to join me.

'There's someone in the house!"

"Where are Nancy and the kids?"

"At Southern States to pick up feed. Lynn and Anne are with her."

"Get in the truck." We pile in.

"What makes you think someone's in the house?"

"The light came on in your bedroom. Someone is moving back and forth in front of the window."

I look to the house. Everything appears normal. I'm just about to say so when I see a shadow cross the upper window.

Who could it possibly be? Burglars would need some sort of vehicle to carry stuff. Not that we have much. Our house is surrounded by acres of fields and trees. The only way to get near it with a vehicle is down our driveway, but there's no strange vehicle at the house.

Maybe it's a vagrant living in the woods. They had to hear me drive in. The lights are all on in the barn. They have to know people are around. Whoever they are, they're pretty brazen.

My instinct is to rush in the house and confront whoever it is. I realize that's not good sense. If something happens to me, the twins would be unprotected.

There's no phone in the barn to call the police. I quickly back up our driveway and head down the road for Peterson's.

As I reach for the phone, Ken advises me that there have been a rash of break-ins in the county recently. There may be even more than one robbery ring operating.

The sheriff responds quickly to my call. His men are on the way.

I leave the twins in safety at the store and head back to the farm to wait for the sheriff. I don't want Nancy to arrive home with the kids and walk into a bad situation.

Coming from the opposite direction, the sheriff and two deputies reach the farm first. All three are well over six feet, and have serious muscles rippling under their tan uniforms. Pistols hang at their waists and rifles are visible in their car. Not a threesome to tangle with lightly. I'm glad they're here.

I introduce myself and watch them go down to the house. I follow their directions and wait in the car at the barn. Right before they breach the back and front doors simultaneously, I see a shadow in the bedroom window.

Whoever it is, they're still in the house.

I can see the deputies moving on the lower floor. Seconds later, the sheriff passes the window where I saw the shadow. I tense. I hope he isn't surprised by a burglar. Any second, I expect to hear shouting.

Nothing happens. At least from what I can see and hear. I'm a nervous wreck by the time the sheriff and his men emerge -- alone.

How can that be?

I know there is someone upstairs. Did they miss the burglar completely?

I hop out of the car and hurry down the driveway to join them. They shake their heads as I approach.

"No. I could see a shadow upstairs when you went in."

"Wait here." They rush back inside, weapons drawn.

A few minutes later, they're back.

"The house is empty."

How can that be? I know what I saw.

"Nothing seems disturbed. Why don't you come in and check if anything's missing?"

Once inside, I'm stunned. I can't see any difference from when I left for work this morning. The house is totally normal. Nothing missing. My eyes dart around anxiously. I don't know what to say. I'd have sworn there was someone here, even minutes ago.

"Could they have gone out the back?"

"No sign of it." Feeling like an idiot, I give my apologies to the sheriff and deputies. Luckily, they take it well.

"Thought we had 'em this time. All the calls we've had before come after the ring has been and gone."

We say goodbye and I drive back to Peterson's for the twins.

The twins rush me as I enter. They're as surprised as I am.

They repeat the same thing I said, "But we saw someone." We load up on sandwich makings and drinks for the weekend.

As we check out, Ken says, "If no one was there, you

probably saw the ghost."

Taylor's and Dana's mouths drop open.

"There's no such thing," I immediately respond.

"Just telling you what the old owners used to tell me. Martha said they had a ghost in the bedroom of the old section of the log cabin."

"That's where we saw the shadow," whispers Taylor.

"This is Virginia. Every old house here has ghosts," Ken says.

I whisk the girls out of the store. I can't believe Ken's telling the girls ghost stories. They don't need to be scared any more tonight.

All Taylor and Dana can talk about on the way home are ghosts. I guess that beats robbers. I try to insert some common sense, but I can tell they aren't listening.

Nancy, Lynn, and Anne are home from Southern States when we get back.

The twins jump right in and tell their version of what happened. There's a lot of emphasis on ghosts. I notice Lynn and Anne absorbing it all. I don't like that.

Normally, if I hear this kind of talk, my instant reaction is to tell them how crazy they sound. But I'm learning to slow my reactions and listen to the kids first. Nancy keeps telling me that children are young, not stupid. I need to take the time to listen and let them express themselves, not to blow them off.

Time and again, the twins, Lynn, and Anne have proven how smart they are. All four impress me with how quickly they learn things.

I notice when Nancy works with the animals that they respond to her because she patiently teaches them rather than trying to force what she wants. I'm starting to think that's an intelligent idea to follow as a father. I'm starting to think of my role as more of a teacher and less of a dictator.

Ghosts are absurd of course. And I don't want Anne and Lynn to hear such talk and believe it. But, in an effort to be understanding, I sit Taylor and Dana down in the living room.

"Tell me why you think there are ghosts," I begin.

"When we were in the barn the bedroom lights came on," Taylor says. "If it wasn't a robber, it must be a ghost."

Dana jumps in, "And there was that shadow moving around." Taylor nods in agreement.

"It's a two hundred and fifty year old cabin," I explain. "There must be problems in the wiring. I'm going to check it out."

Taylor shakes her head, "But the shadows?"

"Probably some sort of optical illusion. There are no such things as ghosts. You know that, right?"

Taylor and Dana are very slow to respond.

Dana, "We know, but..."

I repeat, "There's no such thing as ghosts."

Nancy asks from the doorway, "Are you afraid to be in the house?"

The twins shake their heads quickly. "No, not at all." I hadn't thought of that. I should have.

"You'll tell us if you ever are, won't you?"

Taylor and Dana agree.

**

I'm just drifting off to sleep that night, when Nancy whispers in my ear.

"There are ghosts, you know."

Now I'm awake again. "It's one thing for the girls to believe in ghosts, but not you."

"I know people who have ghosts."

"Of course they do. And they believe in werewolves, vampires, and the tooth fairy, too."

"Can you see radio waves, electricity, magnetism?

"No, but you can measure them."

"Only in the last few hundred years or less. Before that they were unknown."

"That's comparing apples and oranges."

"You're an engineer. What's that saying, energy cannot be created or destroyed, only changed from one form to another? Aren't people comprised of energy?"

"That's a reach, honey."

"No one has disproved the existence of ghosts, have they? There are more things in the universe than man."

"Please stop."

"You know my friend, Carleen, from Leesburg? She lives in an old two-story house. Sometimes when she and her mother are upstairs, they hear a party downstairs on their veranda. They hear men and women talking, the clatter of glasses and cups, laughter, and people moving around. And it's been documented by others and written up in several books."

"Come on. Leesburg goes back to a settlement in the 1730's. The buildings are old, just like our cabin. They make noise."

"Too many people have heard it. And it's always the same. Would you like to go listen?"

"No."

"My friend, Janet, over in Culpeper, her family hears the sounds of cavalry troops riding down their driveway. She also has some malevolent ghosts in her dining room. First they could hear things being slammed against the walls when no one was in there.

They'd run in and find plates and silverware all over the place. Then they'd be eating and knives and forks would lift off the table and hurl into the walls, driving them out. Luckily, not all ghosts are bad like that."

"None of them are, because they don't exist." I get that look again.

"You do remember when my cousin and his wife stayed in our bedroom?

Okay. I remember the visit.

"His wife complained there was something weird about the room and she couldn't sleep."

Hmm. I do vaguely remember that.

23

A CAT BY ANY NAME

My job soon includes trips to places like the Caterpillar Plant in Illinois to discuss computer aided manufacturing. Robots are becoming a major tool in vehicle production lines, which means I'm away an increasing amount.

But one thing I'm learning is that a lot can go wrong on a farm in a single day. I don't like going away and leaving Nancy to deal with it all plus Lynn and Anne. She never complains, but I prefer being there with her myself.

Thank goodness Taylor and Dana are there. I feel better knowing that they're helping Nancy.

I even miss Amy when I'm away. Every night when I come home from work, I find Amy waiting for me at the gate with a stick. This is something new for me. I've come to look forward to our game each evening.

The corn in my garden has grown about a foot high and the other vegetables are several inches high. But the weeds are everywhere and growing faster.

I thought mixing manure into the dirt for fertilizer would be smart. Turns out it wasn't a good idea. I was just spreading around seeds from the hay the horses had eaten and not digested.

Even their straw bedding has some seed in it. Plus the garden is surrounded by fields full of grasses and weeds. With all this competition for space in the garden, I can't keep up with the weeding.

My work travel isn't helping either. Dana and Nancy have put in an hour here and there, but it's not enough. Gardening might soon join the list of things Nancy doesn't do well, like cooking and ironing.

Every weekend I spend a few miserable hours of hot, backbreaking weeding. Maybe a two acre garden is a bit too ambitious.

I walk to the house for a sandwich. In the yard, I see the black barn cat from Curtis' mom. And she's not alone. There are two kittens following her.

Two kittens? How did that happen? Okay, I know how that happened. I mean why did it happen?

I storm into the kitchen and confront Nancy. Lynn's and Anne's eyes grow wide as they look up from their lunch.

"That barn cat is out there with kittens."

"Smitty?"

"Who's Smitty?"

"The barn cat from Curtis' mom. Kittens? That makes sense. We haven't seen her for a week, so we were worried."

"Why wasn't the cat fixed? The vet's here all the time."

"It's my fault. I never thought about it. There's only one cat here."

"Not unless you believe in immaculate conception."

"Where's Lynn?"

136

I turn. Her chair is empty. She's not in the room, and the outside kitchen door is open.

At a year and a half, Lynn is pretty nimble.

Nancy grabs up Anne and we rush outside.

There's Lynn, happily petting Smitty. As we spot her, she reaches for one of the kittens. It hisses nastily, and tries to scratch.

I quickly seize Lynn.

"Kitty," Lynn tells me.

She points at a black kitten with one white foot.

"Wood." What?

"She's calling that one 'Wood,'" Nancy says.

Wood?

"They're wild. Do not touch the kitties." I warn Lynn.

Nancy leaves Lynn and Anne with me and approaches the cats. Smitty likes being petted. The kittens continue to hiss and carry on when Nancy tries to touch them.

"Nice Smitty."

"Why is the cat's name Smitty?" I blurt out.

"Curtis' mom named her. That's why she thought the cat was perfect for us."

What better way to get rid of a cat than to name it after someone and then give it to them as a gift. I'm going to have to keep an eye on Curtis' mom. That's one smart woman.

**

A few months later, I sneak in to check Anne before going to bed. She's sound asleep. I move on to Lynn's room and discover the kitten, Wood, tucked under the blanket with her. Lynn's asleep, but Wood opens his eyes as I approach. I reach in to remove him. He hisses at me. I back up quickly. I don't want to wake Lynn, so I head to Nancy.

"She's got that kitten in bed with her," I say.

"Amazing how kids and baby animals get along."

"That's not what I mean." I get one of those looks. "No cats in the house. That was the deal, remember?"

"I'll put him outside tomorrow. You can have a talk with Lynn."

Hmm. Maybe I should risk the scratches and let Nancy talk to Lynn.

On a hunch, I check Anne's room again. On the far side of her bed, I find the other kitten curled up on a pillow in an open shoe box. Anne wakes up.

"Go back to sleep."

"Mar..."

"What?"

"Mar...Mmmm gooo," she mumbles.

**

As Nancy and I prepare for bed, I have to get it off my chest, "What if those kittens scratch or bite them? It's too dangerous."

"Don't worry so much. Kids and baby animals are fine together as long as the kids aren't abusive, and ours are not."

"What was Anne mumbling - 'Mar...Mmmm gooo?"

"She named her kitten Mary - Mother of God."

"No, that's the last straw. I absolutely refuse to go around the neighborhood calling, "Here, Mary, Mother of God."

24

MISSING

It's been a tough day at work. I drive home in anticipation of stick tossing with Amy. I'm surprised as I park the car. No Amy. I look around. Maybe she's still in the house. I hate to admit that I'm disappointed.

I search for her as I enter. The twins are in the living room playing Monopoly on the floor. I wave. Lynn and Anne rush to me for hugs. Every time I see them, I love them more. Nancy's prepping dinner. More hugs, but no Amy.

"Where's Amy?" Nancy glances around. "I thought she was outside waiting for you. Try calling her."

I do with no success.

Nancy drops what she's doing and goes outside.

The twins catch on that Amy's missing.

"Please stay with the kids. I'm going out and help Nancy. I'm sure everything is okay."

Only it isn't. We check the barn and the main area of the farm. No Amy. It's dark now. Taylor comes out with flashlights and stays to help. Dana stays with the kids.

We all know something is seriously wrong. Even I know Amy would never leave the family.

We walk the driveway and the fence lines. We're not making any progress. At midnight, I call an end to the hunt. We'll start again at dawn.

The twins settle down for the night in the living room. I check Lynn and Anne.

They've both fallen asleep, but Nancy and I can't. I ask her to go over when she last saw Amy again.

"Paul, a friend of a friend from Warrenton, came late this afternoon to see the chestnut horse. He was here about an hour. He didn't think the horse was right for his client. We talked a bit, said goodbye, I came in to fix dinner, and he left. I thought Amy was in the yard."

We already placed a quick call to Paul earlier. He had no help to offer.

Amy's disappearance doesn't make any sense. I can only hope that she'll be at the front door in the morning when we get up.

**

She isn't. It's as if she vanished off the face of the earth. Did she tangle with a wild animal like a raccoon? No one believes she ran off.

We do all the usual things - run ads in the local paper, put up flyers, and knock on our neighbors' doors. We cover every inch of the surrounding area in case Amy's trapped somewhere. Nothing even turns up a lead.

Nancy's inconsolable. Amy would never wander off. She fears the worst.

A sad week later, I head into Peterson's to pick up milk and the usual Yahoos for the twins.

Ken waves me over as I enter.

"I was just about to call you. This is Hank." I shake hands with a wiry guy in his early forties.

"I may have some information about your missing dog." Hank points to the posted picture of Amy. "I seen that dog about six, seven days ago."

"Where?"

"I work up on Route 50 at the welding place."

I nod. I know where that is. It's about a half mile west of where our dirt road meets Route 50 and about two miles from our farm. Route 50 is a high speed, busy highway between Fairfax and Winchester, but it narrows to one lane each way between Arcola and Upperville, the area we're near.

Hank continues. "We was finishin' up for the day. I seen a car across the road stop, a door open, and a dog like that jumped out. He headed east. The car drove off in a hurry."

"She," I correct.

"Huh?"

"The dog is a she."

Hank shrugs.

I realize east would be towards our place.

"What kind of car was it?"

"Didn't pay much attention. It was the dog gettin' out caught my eye."

So, if that was Amy, she would have to be between there and home. Why hadn't she made it yet?

Ken interrupts my thoughts. "There's more."

Hank says, "I kinda watched the dog. It was headed down Route 50 on the shoulder. An' it had almost reached where the first dirt road intersects 50."

That's our dirt road.

"This car headin' west swerved off the road deliberately an' hit the dog. Had to go way off the road to do it. Was disgustin'."

"And the dog?"

"A goner for sure."

"Did you check?"

"None of my business."

"Is she still there?"

He shrugs.

I thank him for telling Ken and me about the dog, buy him a six pack of his favorite Budweiser, and hurry to the door.

I'm filled with mixed feelings. I'm glad for the information, but confused and angry. Who took Amy away in their car? Paul, the man who came to see the horse? A stranger? I wish Hank had noticed more. At least the name and make of the car.

And what kind of demented person drives off the road to hit a defenseless animal. And I'm disgusted with Hank for not checking to see if Amy was still alive. It's been a week. I break the speed limit on my way there to check it out.

And that's where I find her body. Out of sight, part of the way down the slope to the ditch.

I remove a blanket I keep in the trunk of my car and wrap her in it. Tears roll down my face. I'm surprised at my own reaction. I will miss Amy. Amy, who never asked for anything except to be with us. Amy, the Golden Heinz.

I can't bring her back to life, but at least I can bring her home.

We bury her under the oak trees with her favorite stick and a handful of dog bones.

25

BAA BAA BLACK COW

I have a cow. No, not a tantrum. A real four-legged, half Angus, half Hereford steer. He's nine months old and black with a white face.

Ken Peterson heard that someone over in Leesburg was selling all his cattle and let me know. It was still way over my price-to-risk amount, but I figured a way around it. I talked one of my coworkers into splitting the cost with me. It means I only will get half the meat, but it will cut my investment risk in half. I'll use this as a practice year.

Hopefully the steer will work better than my poor garden. The weeds are winning, except around the corn and the tomatoes. Being self-sustaining isn't as easy as it sounds.

At least there's no maintenance on a steer. You point them to the grass and they eat.

"Honey, your cow's here." Nancy interrupts my thoughts.

"That's steer," I correct. I'm juiced. I head toward the barn to greet the man who sold me the steer. Nancy suggested I put him in the small wood paddock behind the barn until he gets used to us. I decide to follow that advice even though the fence there must have been built in the early 1900s. But I think the wood will be safer than our ancient wire fences. I'll feed my steer hay for a while and get him acclimated, before turning him out with the horses. In anticipation of its arrival, I've prepared the paddock with hay, water, and salt.

Clarence and I direct the farmer's trailer back against the big sliding barn doors. The plan is to herd the steer straight through the barn and into the back paddock.

Nancy comes out of the house with Lynn and Anne to watch. Taylor and Dana stand beside her. Even Izzy is here, back from college to board Tony with us for the summer. Disapproval radiates from their direction. I ignore them.

The trailer ramp opens, but the cow refuses to come out. His ex-owner, a burly, balding farmer with what appears to be a perpetual scowl, and a jaw full of chewing tobacco, pushes a broom between the bars and pokes the steer with the brush end. The steer doesn't move an inch. He pats a little harder with no result.

I tell him to hang on a minute with the broom, go into the barn, grab a bucket, and put some grain in it. Then I timidly step into the trailer and rattle the bucket. The steer moves toward me. He's much bigger up close than I thought.

Suddenly he charges.

Dropping the bucket, I leap to the side. The steer brushes past me, knocking me down, and leaps into the barn.

Nancy races up. "Are you all right?"

I nod shakily.

She turns on the ex-owner. "How dangerous is this animal?

"It's not a lapdog, lady. It's a steer. What do you expect?"

144

I can see Nancy's angry.

"Let's get him into the paddock," I interrupt.

We slip into the barn to find the steer's already followed my plan and ended up out in the paddock. I slide the barn door closed behind him.

Nancy puts some more grain in the bucket.

"To help Pork Chop feel at home," she explains.

"Where'd that name come from?"

"Taylor and Dana."

"Very funny, but I think Curtis' mom is still the winner with Smitty."

Nancy ignores me and steps through the back barn door holding the bucket.

As soon as Pork Chop sees her, he charges.

Nancy shrieks, flings the bucket into the air, and dashes for the barn.

I barely manage to shove the door closed in time. Pork Chop slams into it hard, but it holds.

"Hawp, Hawp, Hawp."

We're amusing Clarence.

It's the first time I've ever seen an animal scare Nancy.

"Maybe he'll be calmer when he gets used to us," she says.

But she doesn't sound like she believes it.

I'm having second thoughts. Maybe a steer isn't such a good idea.

26

WHERE'S THE BEEF?

I'm relieved to exit the plane from California at Dulles Airport. Being cramped in coach for five hours is way too long.

Once I collect my bag downstairs and retrieve my car, it's only fifteen more minutes to home. I can't wait to see the family, get out of this business suit, take a shower, and put on some comfy clothes.

While I'm waiting at the luggage carousel, I head for a pay phone to call home.

Two seconds later, Nancy answers.

"Hi, Honey. I'm at Dulles."

"I'm so glad you're back --" I smile at her warm greeting, imagining holding her in my arms as soon as I can ransom my car out of the airport parking lot and get home.

Her voice continues. "--your cow is out, again." She refuses to call Pork Chop a steer, but when she says cow, the local farmers think it's cute. They certainly don't cut me that kind of slack.

"We've been hunting for him all week. I didn't want to mention it while you were away. There's been no sign of him, but

147

one of the neighbors just reported seeing him down by the woods along Route 621."

"That's good."

"Can you take care of it? I'm headed to the doctor's with the kids for their shots."

"Sure." My smile fades. No warm hugs, no shower until later. Bummer.

"Love you. See you later."

Not exactly the homecoming I'd pictured. This is Pork Chop's fifth escape, not including the time he got in my garden and trampled all of the corn. I think he deliberately times his escapades with my business trips. I realize Nancy and the girls are tired of chasing him. It means that all their other plans were scrapped while I was away because of the dangers of the steer being loose. They know if he gets into trouble, someone could be hurt. In addition, we could be sued. Not just us, but also my coworker who owns half of Pork Chop.

I slow down as I pass the woods along 621 on my way home. Maybe I'll catch a glimpse of Pork Chop.

Not a chance. Trees line both sides of the road. The woods are so dense, a black steer could be twenty feet away and totally invisible.

Suddenly, I spot a cow pie on the road ahead. It must be Pork Chop's. How many other cows can there be wandering around loose and pooping in the neighborhood? I pull over to the shoulder and get out.

Big mistake. The second I leave the car's air conditioning, the ninety-five-degree heat hits me, as well as the unbearably high, ninety-eight percent east coast summer humidity. When I left Los Angeles, the temperature was seventy-two with sixteen percent humidity.

I check out the cow pie. Looks soft, so it must be recent. He's got to be close by. I better not take the time to go home and change clothes or he could be in the next county by the time I get back.

Loosening my tie, I open the car trunk. It's packed with odds and ends. After a bit of rooting around, I find what I'm looking for - a long length of rope. I grab it and head into the woods. It must have rained here recently as the ground is muddy.

My clothes stick to my body quickly in the humidity. I wish I'd thought to leave my jacket in the car. Tree branches scratch and tear at me. The rope rolled over my shoulder keeps tangling in bushes.

This is stupid. What am I doing here? Pork Chop could be anywhere.

There's a squishy noise. I look down.

Correction. Pork Chop must be close by. I've discovered another fresh cow pie the hard way. With my new dress shoes. Crap. Literally.

Last night -- a pleasant wine and cheese business party in California. Today --- life as usual, at home on the farm.

Pork Chop is definitely more trouble than I expected when I decided to get a steer.

Ahead there's another cow pie. The dang steer must have diarrhea.

I move forward.

There, in a little clearing ahead, is Pork Chop. He's quietly grazing.

Okay. I actually found him. But maybe I didn't think this through. How am I going to get the rope around his neck? I'm no cowboy. I've never lassoed anything.

Suddenly I remember Nancy approaching a nervous horse. I reach down and snatch a handful of grass like she does.

I step toward the steer with the grass extended.

"Come on, Pork Chop. Come get some nice grass." It's working. He's standing still and looking straight at me.

I'm closer. This is going work. I let the rope slide into my other hand.

The movement makes Pork Chop wheel and canter off.

I dash forward in a desperate attempt to catch him. But I trip --*splat* -- head first into a puddle.

Wiping mud from my face, I catch a glimpse of Pork Chop's tail disappearing into the woods.

Rats. What is it with animals and mud? Does there always have to be mud?

It takes me another half hour of hunting through the woods to get close to him again. This time he's grazing under a tree. Good. The nearby trees provide cover as I slip towards him.

I manage to get within five feet without being seen. Rope ready in my hand, I step out quickly and loop the rope over his head.

"Got'cha." Finally!

"MOO." Abruptly, Pork Chop bolts.

No match for six hundred pounds in motion, I'm yanked after him. It's all I can do to stay on my feet. I can let go at any time, but I'm determined not to.

Pork Chop pulls me deeper into the woods. If I don't do something soon, this could end badly. Mud might be the least of it. Still, I refuse to let go.

I spot an upcoming sturdy tree. By running on an angle

sideways, I get the tree between me and Pork Chop. Circling it with the rope, I try to create an anchor.

The line tightens.

Pork Chop comes to a screeching halt.

The tree wavers slightly, but holds firm.

Annoyed, he turns toward me.

I tug the rope. Pork Chop reacts by pulling as far away from me as he can.

Uh, oh. Now what? There's no way I can lead him. He's apt to give me a one-way ticket to the Emergency Room.

What does Nancy do when she has trouble with those big horses? I try to think.

There was some situation last month. She used a tranquilizer from her medicine chest.

That's it. If I can give him a little tranquilizer, he'll be easy to lead home.

Securing the rope around the tree, I head for the car. When I reach home, I dig through the horses' emergency medical kit in our barn. I find a needle and syringe.

Perfect. Now where's the tranquilizer? Hunting a little further, I locate it.

The dosage is based on weight. I do the math and carefully draw the right amount into the syringe.

Back in the woods, Pork Chop waits, tied to the tree, but on alert. He focuses on me warily.

When I try to approach him, he backs in a circle, keeping the distance between us the same. Then he pauses for a moment. Seeing an opportunity, I lunge forward with the syringe aiming for his butt. Just as I connect, Pork Chop bucks and kicks. I leap back hastily.

I check the syringe. The needle's bent at a right angle and the syringe is empty. I must have totally missed. Damn. Another trip home to the medicine kit for a refill.

When I return with more tranquilizer, Pork Chop backs away again as I approach. This time I notice the rope is winding around the tree trunk, pulling him closer and closer to the tree. If I can get him to keep backing up, he'll be snugged up tight and unable to move when I give him the shot.

For the first time since I got the phone call, a smile crosses my face. I really do have you this time, Pork Chop. Visions of that warm bath, family dinner, and Nancy roll across my mind.

It works perfectly. I step forward, he retreats -- until he's right up against the trunk. I reach around and inject the tranquilizer. This time there's no resistance. He seems tired, too.

I give him some time to let the medicine take effect.

**

A short while later and I'm leading Pork Chop out of the woods and onto the road. It's easy. I did it, I tell myself. Maybe I am getting the hang of this. He's as docile as a lamb. He's even walking nice and slow.

A neighbor drives by and honks as she passes.

I wave back.

She laughs and points behind me.

I turn.

Pork Chop sways with his nose almost on the tarmac.

As I watch in horror, he sinks to his knees.

Then he keels over onto his side with his legs straight out.

Oh no. I've killed him.

I check for a pulse. My life has come to this. Feeling a steer for a heartbeat.

152

Luckily, there is one.

Now what do I do? He's sound asleep.

I prod him with my hands to wake him up. No reaction at all. He's out cold.

It'll be dark soon, and there's no way I can move him on my own. I can't leave him here in the road to go for help. But if I don't go for help, who knows how long I'll be standing here. Definitely catch-22.

Another honk shatters my thoughts. Another neighbor slows down in his battered Ford pick-up truck.

I try to wave him down.

He waves back and drives on. I can see him snickering in his rear view mirror.

Great, I'm going to be the neighborhood joke, again.

Still holding the loose rope, I glance down at the sleeping cow. Pork Chop's sides slowly heave up and down.

There's not a doubt in my mind that this cow was put on earth to torment me. If a black cow is as much bad luck as a black cat, do I need a witch to remove the curse? I guess if I'm forced to burn a black steer at the stake, I can at least have barbeque.

It's another fifteen minutes before the next car passes. Thank goodness it's "rush hour" or it could be hours between cars.

It's Curtis. He slows and stops beside me when I wave. I explain the problem.

"I can head over to your place an' get your trailer," he offers. "Then I can back up next to him an' we'll try to wake him enough to get him loaded."

Sounds good to me. That's a better plan than mine -- since I didn't have one.

Curtis returns with the trailer and we carefully back the ramp

153

to within a foot of Pork Chop. The two of us manage to lift, push, and prod him into the trailer. He's still groggy when I secure the trailer ramp.

It's with relief that I watch Curtis put the pickup in gear and head down the road to our place.

Back at the farm, we open the tailgate, roll him into the barn, and close the doors. We leave him snoozing comfortably and probably counting people jumping over a fence.

Curtis and I head to the house for a cold drink. I can definitely use one, or two.

27

WHEN THE WIND BLOWS

My windshield wipers swing back and forth like a metronome as I head home from work. Hurricane Agnes is approaching. Not a big deal. Hurricanes that reach our area in the piedmont of the Blue Ridge Mountains are generally the equivalent of strong rain storms. Especially this one. It was barely a hurricane when it hit Florida. By the time it crossed Georgia it was already downgraded to a depression. It's true that by the time it made North Carolina, it was back up to a tropical storm, but everyone knows that hurricanes get slower as they cross over land. I'm sure it will be back to a depression long before it arrives here in Northern Virginia. In Arcola, we're a long way from the coast. As I said, no big deal.

I heard some older residents in our area are listening to Curtis' mom. She's saying we should batten down for this one. I mean, really. The woman thinks she knows better than all the weather reporters?

The forward edge of the hurricane should hit the farm later tonight. I decided to come home at four to beat the traffic.

I note Izzy's little red Volkswagen at the barn as I pass it on the way to the house. Seeing it makes me smile. It always reminds me of the little gray Volkswagen Nancy had when we first met. Super Volks, she called it. She had even made up a little rhyme that went with the name.

"Faster than a speeding skateboard, able to leap tall pebbles in a single bounce, and stronger than the mightiest eggbeater -- it's Super Volks." I wonder if Izzy's car has a name too.

Before I reach the house, I see Nancy in the pickup following me down the muddy driveway. She parks beside me. With her are our two kids, Izzy and Dana.

Nancy hands Lynn and Anne over to me.

"Hi, Honey. It was too wet to exercise the horses, so we went down to Fair Oaks Mall for the afternoon. Taylor's home with the flu today."

"I had mud pie for lunch," adds three-year-old Lynn, "and it tasted like ice cream."

"I liked it," comes from two-year-old Anne.

"Sounds good to me," I admit.

"Why doesn't mud pie taste like mud?" Lynn is at that age.

"I think it's called that because it's the color of mud," Izzy suggests.

Lynn accepts this, but I can see her thinking about it. I notice Anne looking at the mud in the yard. We've already learned she likes to check things out for herself. I just hope she doesn't decide to taste any of it.

As I start to warn Nancy, the wind picks up and the rain comes down harder. I race for the house with the kids. I can hear Nancy tell Izzy and Dana, "You'd better head for home."

Izzy lives a half hour away and she's dropping Dana off on

her way.

**

The dinner dishes are done. Lynn and Anne are heading to bed. Clarence is already snoring out in his room. We have flashlights ready if we lose power and extra blankets on all the beds if anyone gets cold. Not that we anticipate anyone being cold as we have oil heat which works even when the power is out.

As the rain slams in sheets against the windows, we're warm and secure inside.

The first call comes at seven.

It's Izzy's dad, Roger. "Is she there?"

My heart stops. "Izzy left here a little after four."

Nancy steps into the room behind me. I mouth, "Roger," to her. Alarm registers on her face.

"They were going to stop at Peterson's on the way," Nancy says.

I repeat that for Roger and add, "Did Dana get home?"

"No," he says. "I already called there."

Nancy suggests, "Call Ken and ask when he saw them. They may have mentioned if they were making another stop."

I pass the info on to Roger and add, "I'll call Ken." I quickly get Ken on the line. He's been working in the store all afternoon and hasn't seen Izzy or Dana.

He goes on, "According to Fire and Rescue people, the two creeks between here and you flash flooded this afternoon." Flash floods in Virginia? I thought that was something that just happened out West.

"Do you know when?"

"First reports came in just after four."

"Are you sure? Both Nancy and I came in about then and the

157

road was fine."

"Positive. Curtis couldn't get home. He said the water was deep and rushing over the road."

"Ken, that's when the girls left here."

"I'll alert the rescue people," he says.

I dial Roger back and Izzy's Mom answers.

"Roger's already headed to Ken's. He spoke with the police out there and heard about the water. They have no report of an accident with a red Volkswagen."

"At least that's good news. Next time you talk to Roger tell him I'm going to head down to the store from this side. I'll meet him there." I grab my coat and two flashlights with extra batteries.

Nancy will alert Ken that I'm on my way to his place and man the phone for updates to and from Dana's parents. I tiptoe past Clarence on the porch and out the door. No need to wake him now. With his poor health, he can't help and I know how upset he'll be when he hears the girls are missing. Better to let him sleep.

I head out into the stormy night filled with dread and terrified it may not end well.

It's pitch black and the rain is so heavy I'm drenched before I get in the car. The weather is much worse than I expected. It's no storm, it's a full hurricane.

I drive out to Route 621 and head south towards Ken's. A distance of only about one and a half to two miles, but I don't get far before I'm forced to stop. The road is covered with huge branches and litter. I park on the shoulder and struggle to get out. So much for the car. Looks like the only way I'm moving forward is on foot.

The storm is definitely worse than predicted. If my hat wasn't tied on and have a brim, I wouldn't be able to keep my eyes open at all. Even using the flashlights, it's hard to see more than a few yards.

The creeks are usually only a few feet wide. To reach the store, Route 621 goes through a long, low cow pasture, crosses the first creek, and then climbs a small ridge.

Then it drops down through another long, low area and crosses a second creek before rising again to the area near the store.

I have to struggle against the storm to make any headway. I finally come to the bend above the first low area and start down toward the creek. It's impossible to hear anything with the wind and driving rain.

Suddenly cold water blasts my legs up to my knees. I try to reverse, but the water knocks me down. On hands and knees I manage to scramble back up the hill.

When I'm above the water, I collapse trying to catch my breath. I fan out the flashlight in a wider arc.

What I can see is numbing. When Ken said the creeks had risen, I didn't envision this.

A torrent of water, as far as the flashlight can stretch, rushes past. I'm still more than a half a football field from the creek bed itself. The water's din rises over everything. Fence posts and tree branches wash by.

I now realize the correct name for those low areas. They're flood plains.

Oh, my God. If the girls are in that horrific water...

I scream their names even though I know it's futile. The wind hurls the sound right back down my throat.

I don't know what I expected. This is a nightmare.

For half an hour, I remain there, motionless and

overwhelmed by the guilt. I could have, should have, stopped them before they left the farm.

Devastated, I turn toward home.

**

The news at the farm isn't any better.

From the store side, Roger and the fire and rescue workers tried to launch a boat across the smaller creek nearest to the store. The sheer velocity of the water drove them back. Finally they managed to rig a rope and cross the creek to the hill.

At that point, they were on the far side of the flood plain that stopped me, but they couldn't see anything. They concluded there was no way to advance and reluctantly retreated to Ken's store. Roger calls before I get home. There's no sign of Izzy or Dana.

We pray the girls have somehow escaped. Since sleep is impossible, Nancy and I curl up in the living room to wait out the storm. At daylight I'll head out again. We hug each other tightly.

Two grim hours later, the front door opens and Izzy and Dana enter, totally exhausted and soaking wet, but safe.

Clarence pokes his head in to see what the commotion is about. He quickly joins the impromptu celebration.

I've never felt such intense relief. Nancy dives for the phone. We know Roger's hunkered down on the floor at Ken's store, ready to go out first thing in the morning.

Joy tingles down the line as he hears the great news. The phone is passed around as calls fly back and forth.

Whatever happened can wait. The girls' survival tops everything.

Nancy hustles the girls into hot baths to warm them up, and then to bed.

She tells me, "Their eyes shut before their bodies hit the

sheets."

Nancy and I cuddle happily on the living room couch and are soon asleep too.

The storm's over before dawn breaks. Around six in the morning, Roger arrives with Dana's brother right behind. I'm the only one up to open the door.

"Let them be," Roger says. "I saw Izzy's car on the way here. We can pull it out pretty easily."

We get the pickup, grab a chain, and head out. I can't believe how normal everything looks on 621 except for dodging the huge downed branches. If you hadn't been out last night in the storm, you would think we'd just suffered a normal rain.

As we enter the flood plain of the first creek and pass the spot I fell in the water, I can see the creek ahead. It's already back in its banks. The road is totally clear, washed clean by the water. Wide puddles dot the fields, but the flood water itself is gone.

Toward the bottom of the plain, I spot Izzy's Volkswagen off the left hand side of the pavement. The road is raised about five feet as it crosses the area and paralleled by with barbed wire fencing on both sides. There's a small area where five trees, a few feet apart, have grown up in the fence line. Izzy's car is jammed against those trees, nose down.

I take a slow look around. This was the only clump of trees in the entire flood plain. If the car had not hit the trees, it and the girls would have been washed away.

Images of the raging flood last night race through my mind. The water had been way higher than the little Volkswagen beetle. How on earth did the girls live through this?

The three of us exchange a silent look. It doesn't take much to read each other's minds.

161

The interior of the car is filled with mud and water up to the rolled down windows. We open the doors to drain out what remains. Once Roger hooks up the chain, the little car comes up easily.

Back at the farm, we drop car near the barn and head inside.

The smell of fresh coffee greets us as we enter the house. Nancy's prepared waffles from her mother's special recipe. It's one of the few things she actually cooks well. Her mom was friends with a couple who ran a waffle house in upstate New York, and they shared the recipe. I've never had waffles to beat them. Nancy's family secret is, in addition to a good recipe, they put bacon inside them while they're cooking.

Maybe not for everyone, but serious comfort food in our family.

Izzy follows Dana into the room. They're both dressed in Nancy's clothes.

"Dad!" Izzy's in her father's arms before he can answer. They step outside for a few minutes. Dana hugs her brother and heads for the phone to talk with her mother.

I can only hope Anne and Lynn never find themselves in such a life threatening situation.

I hug my daughters long and hard as I help them into their seats for breakfast. I can tell they're confused by all the emotion this morning. I make an effort to distract them with milk and the waffles.

Izzy and Roger come back in as we all sit down to eat. I can't say how anxious I am to hear the girls' story.

After a bit, Izzy relates what happened.

"We were headed down 621 toward the store, when we noticed standing water on the road. It seemed shallow so I didn't

162

pay attention because of the rain. I drove on through it. Suddenly the steering failed. The water got deeper and swept the car off the hard top and down into the field."

I'd always heard that Volkswagens could float, I thought.

She continues. "The car stopped against some trees right on the fence line. Dana and I thought we would walk back to the farm for help. But then the water kept rising and it was moving too fast."

Dana nods in agreement as she sips her hot chocolate.

I notice Izzy's scratching her arm as she talks.

"We couldn't open the car doors against the pressure of the water, so we rolled down the windows and climbed up on the roof of the car. It was really slippery and we were scared. We realized we were in big trouble when the water started washing over the roof. Our only hope was the trees. Dana went up one and I grabbed a branch on the next one. Below us the car disappeared under the water. Dad, is there any way we can save it?"

"I don't know. We can put a new motor in, but it might not be worth it."

Her car probably saved their lives by floating and hitting the trees. If it had been a heavier car, it would have driven further along the road before it was stopped. They would have been past the trees and surrounded by nothing except rising water. Rest in peace, beloved little red Volkswagen. You did your best.

Wow. Did I just think that? Nancy must be rubbing off on me. Now I'm giving cars human attributes.

Izzy continues, "We climbed higher as the water kept rising. Long after dark, it leveled off, but the noise was deafening. We sat on branches next to each other with our feet in the water. Poor Dana sat in a pine tree and it was itchy."

163

But I notice it's Izzy who's scratching again, harder.

"We sat there for hours in the dark surrounded by the water. We prayed the trees wouldn't fall. We made a plan to hold onto the trees if they did, so we could float. Dad, it was awful."

Roger gives her another hug.

After a minute she goes on. "Finally the rain stopped. Then, just as fast as the water came up, it went down. We waited a while to make sure it was really gone. Then we climbed down and walked back here."

"You two should be very proud," Nancy says. "Keeping your heads in that situation."

We all agree. Not everyone would have made the good survival decisions they did.

"I'm going to make a new farm rule. Everybody stays home for the next hurricane. No shopping, no driving."

Nods all around.

"Drat," says Izzy, I left my new jacket where I sat in the tree." She scratches her leg.

I have to ask her, "Are you all right?"

"I guess."

Nancy has her roll up her sleeve and pants. Izzy's covered with an ugly rash.

Nancy looks closely. "That's poison ivy or poison oak."

Dana giggles. "I sat in a pine tree. You sat in poison ivy."

Nancy takes her upstairs to find some calamine lotion.

When Izzy returns, she says ruefully, "There's no place I don't have poison ivy."

We can't help it. We all laugh. It's great to end the terror of last night on a funny note.

**

Later in the day, I drive Nancy to show her where the kids had been caught. As we look at the trees, we notice a jacket wedged high on a branch. It's over twenty feet up in the air.

"That's Izzy's new jacket," Nancy whispers.

As we look carefully, there's trash on every tree trunk up to the same height. The kids said their feet were in the water, so the water had been that high.

Standing there in the daylight under normal conditions, it was hard to imagine how scary it had been for the girls. They had been very smart and very, very lucky.

28

MY KINGDOM FOR A HORSE OF A DIFFERENT COLOR

I'm in serious trouble.

Nancy left me in charge of the farm for the weekend. She's off to a show with one of the young rescue horses. Izzy and her horse and Taylor are with her.

Clarence is away, too. Dana's here with the kids, but she can't leave them to help me.

My problem is that the horses are outside the barn, waiting to come in for their breakfast.

I'm on my own again for the first time since having to turn out Junior, Bear, and Skinny in Great Falls when Nancy was pregnant. Those were the good old days. There were only three horses back then.

Nancy left long, careful instructions, with diagrams of which horse goes in which stall, but there's a big problem.

Five of the current eight are the same bay color.

I guess it never occurred to Nancy that there would be a problem.

Figgy's white. He's easy. There's a huge chestnut named Bodonis with a white stripe on his face. I can spot him. There's also a new, smaller liver colored chestnut named Boozy Bruce. Honest. That's what his thoroughbred papers record as his official name. I think the boozy one was the person who named him. Those three I can tell apart. All the rest are mid-sized bays.

According to Nancy's list, they're Junior, Masquerade, Ernie, the Three-Year-Old, and the Five-Year-Old. There'd be one more bay, but that's the one Nancy took to the show. I think I know which one is Junior, but no way I can tell the other ones with names apart, much less a three-year-old and a five-year-old.

If they all ate the same amount, it wouldn't matter if I put them in the wrong stalls. Unfortunately, their meals and additives vary greatly. I'd have to get the right horse with the right meal even if I screw up which stall they're in.

Eight pairs of annoyed equine eyes follow me as I leave them standing outside the barn and head back to the house.

In my head, I can hear Figgy muttering, "Come back. I want my breakfast." And I'm sure Junior's thoughts are unprintable.

As an engineer, I believe in using available resources. I have only one.

Dana.

I put her in my car with Lynn and Anne and park it next to the barn entrance. I don't want our two little kids on the ground while the horses are milling around.

As I bring each horse past the car, Dana tells me which horse it is and what stall it goes in. Problem solved.

If they wore halters, I could attach name tags, but that would be way too easy. Nancy doesn't believe in leaving halters on horses. When they're turned out or in their stalls, she removes them. She's

168

heard of too many horses scratching their ears or their face with a hind foot and getting the foot hung in their halters. Once a horse is caught in an awkward position like that, he will panic, often falling over and injuring himself. So if Nancy must leave a halter on one for some reason, she uses a very thin leather one that will stretch or break free if enough pressure is put on it. I only wish there were a way I could paint the horses' names on their butts, but somehow I don't think she'll go for that.

Nancy's consistent. When Amy was alive, she rarely wore a collar either. She'd had all her tags and shots, but living in the country, dog collars can be a death trap for a dog. Apparently it's a rural thing. A dog squeezing through a wire fence can catch his collar on some protrusion and get stuck. Or going through a wooded area, a branch can catch under its collar. If you can't find the dog and release it in time, it will starve to death. Local hunting dogs are tattooed inside their thighs since they don't wear collars either.

All that's great for the animals' safety, but no help to me in this situation.

As soon as the horses are in and eating, I drive Dana and the kids to the house.

Then I head back to the barn to finish up. If my automatic feeders and waterers had worked, the chores would be a lot faster and easier.

I pour dry cat food in their tack room bowl for Smitty, Wood, and Mary, Mother of God.

After the cats, I throw hay into Pork Chop's paddock and shove a bucket with grain under the fence so he can reach it. I don't dare go in the paddock with him. He hasn't become any tamer in spite of our efforts.

169

As I'm cleaning water buckets and refilling them, I notice Junior hasn't touched her breakfast. I know it's Junior because I taped index cards with all the horses' names outside their stalls. I run my hand through her feed tub to see if there's a problem, but I don't see any reason for her not to be eating. The other horses are already licking the bottom of their tubs.

I decide I'll check on her later. I don't know how you tell if a horse is sick, so I better ask when Nancy calls tonight. If I'm going to have a problem with any horse, of course it will be Junior.

"Hello, anyone here?" Just what I need. It's Vance, the most persistent of the real estate agents.

"There you are," he says when he spots me.

"Morning." I try to keep the annoyance out of my voice.

"I was in the area and thought I'd stop by. Did you make a decision on the price you'll sell your property for?"

"Nothing's changed. We're not interested in selling." This guy really irritates me.

"Come on, Brad. There has to be a figure that would make you happy? Just name it."

"Vance, I wouldn't sell this place unless you come back with a no contingency contract for double what we paid." There. That should keep him off my back.

"I have your word on that?"

"Sure."

"Thanks. I'll be seeing you."

Sure you will.

I wish I'd thought of saying that earlier. It's a perfect way to get rid of all the pesky agents.

I yawn as I finish up. I'm looking forward to some hot coffee and my breakfast.

I notice Bodonis yawn, too. I never knew horses yawned. I guess he's getting ready to go to sleep after being out all night grazing. It's not unusual to come in the barn during the summer days and find half of the horses lying down. We even had one ex-racehorse that snored loudly. The first time we heard him, we thought he was dying.

**

By Sunday night, I'm pretty proud of myself. The weekend has gone smoothly.

Junior's lack of appetite was solved when Nancy called last night.

"I should have warned you. If the trailer leaves and Junior's not in it, she pouts and doesn't eat. Just have Clarence run his hand through her feed. Then she'll eat it."

What? My hand isn't good enough? Besides, Clarence is away for the weekend.

"Does that also explain the other weird thing Junior did today? While she was waiting to come in, I noticed her go over where you park our trailer next to Izzy's trailer.

The ramp was still down from when Izzy had last cleaned and hosed hers out. Junior stepped halfway into the trailer, turned around, looked straight at me and whinnied."

"Clarence tells me she's done that when I go to shows without her. She really doesn't like to be left home."

After the call, I get an idea. I grab Clarence's old jacket from the hook beside the door and walk back up to the barn with it. When I look in Junior's feed tub, her dinner is still untouched. I wave Clarence's jacket over her dinner. Almost immediately, Junior comes over to inspect what I'm doing. Putting her head in her feed tub, she starts munching away.

Go figure.

I can hear Clarence's response now. "Hawp, hawp, hawp."

**

All I have left to do with the horses is turn them out for the evening. Nancy, Izzy and Taylor will return an hour or so after that.

As I enter the barn, I yawn. It's been a long day. I see Bodonis yawn, too. Just like yesterday.

Curious, I experiment by pretending to yawn again. So does Bodonis. I repeat it.

Right on cue, he does too.

I stand in front of Figgy's stall and pretend to yawn. Figgy looks at me like I'm nuts and doesn't move a hair. Okay. He doesn't want to play.

I try again in front of Ernie. On my second one, he yawns. This is cool.

I test all of them. Bodonis, Ernie, Boozy Bruce and the five-year-old will all yawn when I do.

Tonight, I'm laughing as I turn the horses out. Wait 'til I tell Nancy. She'll get a kick out of it.

Done, I head into the tack room to check if the cats need more food.

SLAM! The tack room door shuts behind me.

I guess a breeze caught it. I haven't closed the main barn door yet.

But when I go to push it open, it doesn't budge. How on earth could it be locked?

"Hello. Is anyone there? Dana?"

No answer. I peek through the vertical crack between the door and the wall. I can see the metal closure bar across the gap.

172

How could that possibly happen?

A white blur passes outside the gap.

Oh, no.

Figgy.

He must have come back into the barn.

The slide bolt and latch on the tack room is the same as the ones on the stalls that he's been known to open. Only the tack room has no windows, the door isn't Dutch, and there's no way to open it from inside.

I'm trapped.

Damn Figgy. Did I annoy him with the yawns?

Dana won't know I need help. Oh, my gosh. I'm stuck until Nancy comes home in a couple of hours. At least I know she, Taylor, and Izzy have to come to the barn to put away the two horses they have with them.

I search the tack room for any kind of useable tool to force the door. There's nothing. I sit down to wait, vowing to rework the door first thing when I get out.

This is going to be totally embarrassing.

29

BAD DOG

Breakfast is over and Nancy has already gone to the barn when Taylor shows me the classified ad in today's paper: Home wanted for a male (neutered) Dalmatian.

Dana and Taylor are helping me secretly search for a new dog for Nancy. No dog can replace Amy, but I know that her loss left a hole in our family. I also don't want Nancy and the girls to be alone on the farm while I'm away on business. A big dog will provide some security.

The twins have been calling around to the local county pounds checking for an appropriate dog. While they enjoy the project, they're not finding anything suitable. But this ad caught Taylor's eye.

She watches me hopefully as I read the details.

Two-year-old male Dalmatian. Healthy. Looking for a good home. Altered is good. The ad certainly leaves a lot to the imagination. Still...

"This might be good. Nancy mentioned that her family had Dalmatians when she was little. She likes them. Would you like to

175

call and see if we can make an appointment this afternoon to see it?"

Pleased, Taylor heads for the phone.

I head to the barn to broach the subject with Nancy.

"No, it's too soon," is her first response.

I mention the contents of the ad.

"That's sad. I doubt anyone wants an adult dog. He'll end up at the pound," Nancy says. "I wonder why they're giving him up."

I know she's hooked. We're going to see the dog.

Lynn, four, and Anne, three, won't be back from visiting with a neighbor's kids for several hours. That means all four of us, Nancy, Taylor, Dana, and I, can check out the dog.

In the car, Taylor reveals that the woman she spoke with hadn't answered any questions. She just said come and see him. That worries me again. I'd hate to waste our Sunday afternoon.

"We'll know soon enough," Nancy says.

We locate the right street in Sterling, a nearby planned residential community.

Each house has a quarter acre lot. Although similar, one-story ranchettes, the houses aren't identical. I stop the car in front of a neat little house at the right address. It has a chain link fence and a tricycle sits on the driveway.

Nancy notes the tricycle. "Good sign. The dog is used to kids."

I ring the doorbell and hear a deep bark from inside.

A thin, tired woman in her late twenties opens the door a crack.

"Come on in. I'm Fern."

Coming in is difficult because she barely opens the door far enough for us to singly squeeze through. I look at Nancy and shrug.

Inside we take seats on a hard, plaid sofa, and Fern goes to fetch the dog.

Seconds later, she's dragged back into the room by sixty-five pounds of surging muscle.

The dog is huge and he lunges his way toward us. Even I can see Fern is afraid, and clearly can't manage the dog.

Alarmed, I move in front of Nancy, but she waves me aside.

She holds her hand out, low and palm up. I have visions of the beast ripping it off and swallowing it in one enormous gulp.

The dog reaches Nancy's hand and sniffs. Nancy tells him what a good dog he is and pets him. He rubs his head against her. I should have known. Dogs like her.

"What's his name?"

"Shakey."

"What a good dog you are, Shakey. Good boy."

Shakey's tail wags. I swear he smiles, but dogs don't smile.

Fern sighs deeply and collapses into a nearby chair.

"Why don't you tell us about Shakey?" Nancy asks as she continues to pet and talk to the dog.

"Our little girl had this stuffed toy Dalmatian puppy from the movie *101 Dalmatians*. She loved that toy so much that we bought Shakey from a breeder for Christmas. He was the cutest little puppy. Then he grew up. We had no idea Dalmatians got so big. He's just too much for us. My husband and I both work. Our little girl goes to daycare. When we come home and open the door, he bolts past us, jumps the fence, and disappears for hours. We're just too tired to chase him every night."

Great. The dog's a runaway. Like I don't have enough trouble with Pork Chop and Figgy. This dog is a nonstarter.

Taylor and Dana are petting the dog now.

"What does he do when he's out?"

"He never hurts anybody or other animals, but our neighbors complain. We just don't know what to do."

"How was he in obedience class?"

"We don't have time for anything like that."

So the dog is totally untrained. Even I know that's not good.

Fern's six-year-old enters the room with her husband.

"Mommy, Mommy!"

Shakey leaps up and rushes to her. Happy to see the child, he exuberantly jumps on her. The little girl goes down hard. Startled, she bawls.

I can see Nancy's appalled. So am I. I can't believe they let the dog jump on their kid. No way is this dog coming back to our house and doing that to our little girls.

I stand, ready to leave. Before I can speak, Fern introduces us to her husband, who picks up the little girl and wipes her tears.

After the introductions, Nancy says, "The dog is lovely, but I'm not sure he'll fit in with our family."

Perfect, I think. We're in total agreement. We're out of here.

"If it's okay with you, we'd like to take Shakey for a two week trial period."

What? She didn't say that, did she?

"If he doesn't fit in, we'll bring him back."

No, no. Let's skip the two weeks and just leave him here.

I won't say Fern and her husband are thrilled to see Shakey go, but they're waving goodbye before I can protest.

Shakey sits happily in the back seat between Taylor and Dana. I sit unhappily behind the steering wheel.

"Why?" I ask Nancy, "The dog is a maniac."

"Look at him. He's a beautiful dog. There's nothing mean about him. I'm hoping he's as smart as he looks."

"Not to mention he's really great at knocking down little girls."

"I certainly hope we can stop that."

"It's not worth the risk."

"Let's just see what happens, okay? There's no way I'll let him jump on the kids."

I'm not happy, but I don't want to argue any more in front of Dana and Taylor.

When we get home, Nancy takes Shakey on a leash for a walk up to the barn and around the fields. Taylor and Dana tag along, watching and listening. I can see she's talking to the dog.

Shakey starts out distracted by everything around him. Slowly he pays more and more attention to Nancy.

She brings him back to the house just as Lynn and Anne arrive.

"New dog," they say in unison rushing toward Nancy and Shakey.

Shakey bolts toward them until he hits the end of his leash, and I'm too far away to stop him.

Nancy puts her hand up to stop the kids. She grabs Shakey's muzzle in one hand, looks him in the eye, points her finger at him, and says no. He stands stock still.

Then she motions for the kids to come on slowly. They don't. They rush forward.

Nancy says "no" to the dog just as the kids reach them. He doesn't move. As they pet him and ask his name, he licks their faces. Either he really likes kids, or he's cleaning up the remains of their lunch.

He looms over Lynn and Anne. I hadn't realized he's so much bigger than Amy.

Yet Anne and Lynn aren't fazed at all. They're giggling and petting him like they've known him forever.

I swear I see the corners of Shakey's mouth curl up.

Nancy gives Taylor and Dana thumbs up. I can see the pride in their faces. I bite my tongue. I hate to see them all get so excited, but I know this dog is not staying.

30

IN A ONE PONY OPEN SLEIGH

Figgy irks me. Every time I see him I'm steamed that he locked me in the tack room. Nancy refrained, but Taylor and Dana giggled over it for weeks afterward. I've even caught Izzy grinning when she thought I wasn't looking. At least she's gone back to college.

We had the first snowstorm two days ago, and already all the kids have cabin fever. Taylor and Dana teach our girls to play Old Maid in the living room.

Shakey sleeps nearby. Yes, he's still here. And he's never once jumped on the kids or run away. Nancy claims he's a great dog, he just needed someone to tell him no. We'll see.

Nancy pops her head in the door and asks for Taylor. The two whisper outside for a moment, then Taylor grabs her coat and heads through the snow to the barn with Nancy. It's sunny and clear out.

I'm planning next spring's garden. I think half an acre instead of two acres might be easier to manage. And I'm looking for an inexpensive tractor. That way I won't need to pay Curtis every time

I need the garden plowed or the driveway graded. I could even clear snow.

Wood, the kitten, startles me as he charges past. He's going so fast he's almost a blur.

Two seconds later, he dashes by in the opposite direction.

When he passes back again, I follow him.

He's literally bouncing off the walls. First off one wall, then across the room, off that wall, and then back. He's like a wind-up toy wound way too tight. He's cutting right through the living room. I don't understand why none of the kids are paying any attention.

"What's with the cat? Is he sick?" Lynn looks up. "Wood fit."

"He's just running off energy. He'll quit in a minute," Dana adds.

"He's not supposed to be in the house." I'm about to repeat myself when Nancy sticks her head in the door again.

"Can you put coats on the kids? We have a surprise out here." Before I can ask any questions, she's gone. Now what?

We hurry outside as soon as the kids are ready, but nothing could have prepared us for Nancy's surprise. She's rigged Figgy up to a kid's sled.

It's actually quite clever. Taylor is mounted on Figgy. He's wearing a breast plate and Nancy has attached what looks like a tow rope for water skiing from each side of his girth and back to a wooden bar, like the kind you use to water ski.

Nancy sits on the sled with her feet braced against the front cross bar. She places Lynn between her legs. When she's ready, she signals Taylor. Taylor gives Figgy a chirp and off they go around the yard. First at a walk, then at a trot.

The kids are ecstatic.

After a few minutes, Nancy trades off with Dana and Anne. She joins me to watch.

"I wasn't sure if Figgy would do this, so Taylor and I walked him around by the barn to see if he'd freak out. It didn't bother him a bit. He's only connected to the sled by the tow rope, so you just drop the rope if there's a problem."

"Great idea. Look at the smiles on everybody's faces. I'm going for the camera."

Figgy trudges around the yard all afternoon to everyone's pleasure. He never puts a foot wrong. He poses for pictures. He doesn't react to all the yelling and the singing of "Jingle Bells." He's patient, he's willing, and I'd swear he's having a good time, too.

When Nancy asks if I'd like to try it, I lift Anne and we take our places on the sled. With a signal from Taylor, Figgy trots off. I laugh out loud. It's as much fun as it looked.

That night I turn to Nancy as we prepare for bed. "Figgy was fun today. He made us all pretty happy. I think I'll have to forgive him for locking me in the tack room."

"You have to admit, it was pretty funny."

Et tu, Nancy?

31

HORSES-R-US

The day starts pleasantly. Spring is definitely here. Almost time to plow my new, improved half-acre garden with the old International Harvester Cub tractor I just purchased. It's a 1941 model and it's older than I am, but it works great.

Last year's garden was a failure. It would have been far cheaper to buy the small amount of corn and tomatoes that made it to the kitchen table. I had no idea how much work farming really is. Still, I'm committed to my idea to grow food.

As always, it was Ken who told me about the tractor. If Ken got a fee for all the deals he's put together, he'd be a rich man. Several times I've offered him a finder's fee in appreciation, but he was so offended, I don't do it anymore.

The oak trees in the front of our property are all budded with new leaves.

There's no undergrowth except the dogwoods, now in full bloom. Their white flowers spread around the taller oak trunks like skirts. From the house they appear so lovely that I'm drawn to take a walk and see them more closely.

Standing beside the oaks' huge trunks, I'm reminded of the former owners and their concern for these magnificent trees. They needn't worry. No one will touch them as long as we live here.

I move further into the woods, pausing where Amy's buried. Crunch. I hear a noise behind me. It's only Junior. Her field includes the area with the oaks.

Uh, oh. "Only Junior" is a contradiction. She's not grazing aimlessly, she's heading straight for me.

Junior is a funny shape from the front these days. Kind of like a vertical fork with a hardboiled egg sideways in the middle. Nancy and Sharon bred her last year before Sharon moved. She's due sometime this month.

But I'm too anxious to laugh. I remember Junior and the mud puddle. What's she up to now?

I move behind one of the trees. I'll be safe as long as there's a nice, big tree trunk between us.

Not good. Junior stops on the other side of the tree. What's she doing?

I risk a look.

BAM. Junior bumps me in the shoulder with her muzzle and runs behind a nearby oak. As usual, only her head is hidden.

Was she trying to bite me? I never heard that she bit people. I know Nancy won't keep a deliberately aggressive horse.

Junior peeks at me from behind her tree like she does when Nancy wants to catch her. She ducks back when she sees me looking. Is this one of her games?

I slip toward Junior and tap her on the rump. Then I dash behind the nearest trunk.

Junior comes after me and she's faster than I am. She touches my butt lightly with her nose and runs for cover again. Not that there's any cover big enough.

I get it. She's playing tag.

Nancy and Sharon told me she plays games. I never paid much attention. I never heard of horses doing that.

Except maybe Junior.

I run over and touch her neck with the same result. This is kind of fun. We play for another fifteen minutes. Amazing. I never imagined you could do this with a horse.

Junior's quick, even in her condition. She spins and ducks like a professional basketball player. And she's very careful when she touches me.

Maybe all the Junior stories are true.

Finally worn out, I leave the trees and head for the house. Junior senses our game is over and drops her head to graze.

What a perfect spring day. I whistle and glance around as I walk. The horses are busy enjoying the new grass coming up, except for a couple who are lying down, napping in the warm sun.

Wait a minute. There seem to be an awful lot of horses.

I pause to count them. One, two...eight. But that's only the front field.

There are six in the front paddock. Looks like twelve in the back field.

That's...twenty six! How on earth? That can't be right. I count again.

Oh, no. Twenty-six horses. And that's not counting Izzy's horse that's back at school with her.

How is that even possible? We only have nine stalls. Where did they all even come from?

Just wait until Nancy gets home. There's no way we can afford this. It's totally crazy.

Honk! I turn around. It's Vance, that real estate agent has driven in again. I can't believe it. He has no business here.

I storm toward the gate to give him a piece of my mind.

Vance steps out of his car and waves.

He's all smiles when I reach him, aggravating me even more. These guys have no shame.

"Vance, I thought I told you not to come back-"

"-unless I had a contract for double the price. I know, I know. Well, guess what? I have the papers right here, ready to sign. Just like you asked."

Uh, oh.

32

NANCY HAS A COW

This time it's going to take more than a water fight to get me out of the trouble I'm in. We have twenty-six horses and I sold the farm? I don't know which is worse, but Nancy clearly has her priority.

The yelling and name-calling goes on late into the night.

She hasn't said the "D" word yet, as in "Divorce," but I'm afraid with every breath it's next.

"You have twenty-six horses," didn't even get a pause more than, "I told you we were getting more horses. You agreed."

To be fair, I did.

I make a serious note to be more careful about leaving future agreements open-ended. That is, if I manage to survive long enough to make another agreement.

I should have told her when I made the deal with Vance, but it seemed such an impossibility that I hadn't bothered.

Now we have four months to move. It took forever to find this place. How long will it take to find a new one? We can't even afford to board the horses out while we're trying to find a place. At one hundred dollars a head, even a month would bankrupt us.

In addition, I have a couple of work trips scheduled over the upcoming months. I wish I could have reneged on the contract, but I gave Vance my word. He played fair. But where does that leave us?

I head out to the yard. Maybe playing ball with Shakey will make me feel better.

Shakey happily bounces out to the yard with me. I throw the ball.

Shakey stands still beside me and watches it bounce across the back yard.

"Go. Get the ball."

He doesn't move.

I retrieve the ball. I throw it as hard as I can.

"Go on, Shakey. Get the ball."

He just looks at me and wags his tail.

Okay. Maybe he likes sticks better. I search under the trees and find a good one.

"Look, Shakey." I wave it in front of his face. I throw it as far as I can.

He doesn't move.

Great. Even playing ball is a bust.

**

I'm relieved when Nancy turns her attention to the move. She's still not thrilled with me, but she's trying to move on. I know, bad pun.

"We'll need more than nine stalls."

"How many?"

"Let's do twelve. I'll try to sell as many horses as I can before we move."

Sounds like a plan to me. It's a good time for Pork Chop to head off to market when we move, too.

"What if we can't find a place in time?" That's the question.

The phone rings. It's Nancy's mother. As I head upstairs, I hear Nancy trying to explain that we haven't found a new place to live yet. If anyone worries more than Nancy, it's her mother.

At dinner, Nancy tells me why her mother called.

"Mom and Dad were at their church dinner last night and she overheard a woman saying that her friend's children were searching for a place in Loudoun County to buy."

Loudoun County is where we live. So?

"Turns out the woman's friend is the mother of one of my good friends from high school. My friend's married now and that's who's property hunting. I haven't seen her in ages. It'd be nice to have them over for dinner." Nancy's friend is also named Nancy. In school, friends solved the problem simply. My Nancy was Nancy and her friend was Nan.

We fall easily into the same pattern when we have Nan and her husband, Jim over. I can tell it's going to be fun knowing a couple our own age with a farm in the area. Dinner turns out to be a success even though Nancy burns the popovers.

Nan is a special education teacher and Jim is a technician for an electronics manufacturer. They're looking for about ten acres for themselves and their two horses.

Jim outlines their plan to buy land and then live in a trailer until they put up a pre-fabricated house.

We haven't thought about buying undeveloped acreage and building. In fact it probably won't be possible in our limited time. But Jim plants the idea in my mind.

They've been having the same bad luck we originally did. In

191

turn, we share how we found our current place.

We decide to combine our property search and drive around together. Hopefully we can find properties in close proximity. Luckily, Nancy is so excited to catch up with Nan that she forgets momentarily about my selling the farm.

I'll have to remember to use a distraction if I get in trouble again. Of course, if we manage to stay together, a next time is inevitable.

33

RODEO DAZE

"Honey, your cow is out." Words I've come to hate hearing at the end of a long business trip. I don't know how Pork Chop knows, but I swear he waits until I go away before he takes off. We should spend every minute searching for a new farm. That makes the interruption even more annoying.

This time I'm lucky. I, and almost everyone else in the area, know exactly where he's gone.

There's a big property about a mile away on Route 621, near where the girls were caught in the hurricane. The hundred acres of pasture is leased out to a man who grazes his herd of fifty Hereford cattle there. Right smack in the middle of his cattle is Pork Chop.

It's a bit like an ostrich with his head in the sand. He may think we can't see him, but he's hard to miss. Herefords are red with white faces. Pork Chop is black with a white face. He stands out like a beacon.

Jim offers to help when he hears about our Pork Chop problem.

As soon as I get home and change into old chinos, I call to tell him.

"Wait 'til Saturday," he responds. "I'll bring my quarter horse, Stinky, and I'll rope him for you."

Stinky? Do I really want to know where he got that name? I resist the temptation to ask.

Okay. I'm impressed. Nancy says Jim is an excellent rider, and apparently he can rope as well. I think he might be the answer to my prayers. I have no problem waiting.

Saturday afternoon at the appointed time, Jim parks his horse trailer on the side of Route 621 right behind our trailer. Inside ours is Figgy. Nancy decided to ride out with Jim and try to keep Pork Chop moving in a straight line while Jim ropes him.

Exactly like they do in steer roping contests in rodeos.

Taylor and Dana insist on coming and therefore Lynn and Anne are there with them. The four of them will have a good vantage point from the fence line.

We unload Figgy and Stinky. No one knows what Figgy will think of being a cow pony.

When I ask Nancy, her response is, "Why not? He does everything else."

With Nancy mounted on her English saddle and Jim on his western one, I open the gate and they ride into the field.

Jim loosens his lariat and takes a few practice swings. Figgy ignores the rope completely.

When Jim nods, they move quietly and patiently into the herd. The cattle part to let the ponies through. I don't know if Pork Chop recognizes Figgy and Nancy, but he slowly weaves away from them, from the middle of the herd to the farthest edge. Somehow he knows they've come for him.

194

For about twenty minutes, Jim, with Nancy nearby, quietly stalks Pork Chop to no avail. The steer constantly maneuvers to keep several Herefords between him and the riders.

Jim decides to change tactics. The ponies move to a trot.

The herd resents the faster intrusion and moo in protest as they jump out of the way.

Jim and Stinky try to cut Pork Chop away from the other cattle. Nancy follows closely. I'm sure Jim would be fine by himself, but Nancy is anxious to help.

For another fifteen minutes, Pork Chop manages to evade them, still using the other cattle as a buffer. Jim tries to be careful not to upset the herd. The unknown owner would not be appreciative. Our steer doesn't have the same concerns.

Suddenly Jim finds the break he's looking for. Stinky surges forward, effectively cutting Pork Chop off from the other cattle.

Jim's lasso swings.

A roar goes up on the road. Startled, I look around. I've been following the action, so I hadn't noticed the cars are stopped up and down the road. Neighbors, along with people I've never seen, line the roadside, watching.

A groan follows the cheer. Pork Chop dodges the rope at the last second.

Jim persists. Pork Chop ducks and dodges. Nancy and Figgy try to get the steer to run in a straight line. They zigzag back and forth across the pasture with Jim trying to get a clear lasso shot and Pork Chop doing his best to cut back into the herd.

A gasp from the crowd. Pork Chop trips in a depression and goes down. Jim and Nancy pull up hard.

This part, I hear from Nancy later.

Jim waits by the steer for him to get up. Nancy notices Jim's not doing anything.

"Quick. Get him now."

"It's not fair to rope him while he's down." Pork Chop is moving his legs under him to get up.

"This is not about being fair. Catch him."

Reluctantly, Jim drops the rope over the steer's head and pulls the loop closed.

There's applause from the crowd.

Startled, Jim and Nancy look up and notice the people for the first time.

It's nice to know we entertain the neighborhood.

With the rodeo over, the crowd thins out quickly. Jim and Nancy are a long way from the gate to the road. They walk back slowly, cooling the ponies out and making sure Pork Chop is okay.

On their way, they come around the raised rim of a large pond. Forced to ride single file, Jim and Stinky in front, leading Pork Chop behind them. Jim has his end of the rope securely tied to his saddle horn. Nancy and Figgy follow. They're all on the rim, when Pork Chop drifts to the right, away from the pond.

I hear a yell from Nancy.

Pork Chop turns at a right angle facing the pond. Suddenly he gathers himself to launch into the water. If his weight gets into the air, he'll take Jim and Stinky at the other end of the rope, in with him.

Alerted, Jim uses his quick reflexes to drag on the rope, successfully making the steer turn his head back toward Stinky's hindquarters.

They make it back to the gate with no more incidents. We manage to get Pork Chop loaded in our trailer. Figgy will ride home with Jim and Stinky.

Now that we're done, I breathe a sigh of relief.

34

OH, GIVE ME A HOME

After weeks of touring the countryside, Nancy, Nan, Jim, and I stop at Ken's for gas and a cold drink. We chat a bit with Ken while the gas pump runs.

"You know, I seem to remember one of the people up on 621, a mile or so past you, Brad. The Youngs, Quint and Pat. They were talking about selling off nine or ten acres a while ago. Why don't you go talk with them? See if they still want to sell."

And Ken does it again. The Youngs have a nine-plus acre lot to sell. The front part is open field, peppered with small cedar trees. Then the land rolls downhill into a wooded area with a creek. It suits Jim and Nan well and they buy it.

While driving to the Youngs' property I notice again a battered for sale sign covered with vines on an open field next to Route 621. It's about a half a mile from Jim's and Nan's new place. When I'd asked about it a couple weeks ago, I'd been told it was marshy and only good for pasture. But as we keep driving past, I wonder if I should take a look myself.

Encouraged by Jim and Nan's success, Nancy and I continue

searching, but with no luck. We're starting to panic as time drifts away. The contract on our log cabin is a no contingency one as I'd insisted.

We could find ourselves with twenty-four horses out on the street. Nancy's only sold two. Pork Chop is gone too, leaving me with mixed feelings.

One day, driving up 621, I see the battered sign again. Not being in a hurry, I park and get out. Peeling back the vines, I find a diagram of the property. It's a big rectangle. One side fronts right on 621. As I remove more vines, I read that it's forty acres. Double what we want, but maybe they'll sell us half.

I walk around. Yes, the left hand front side near the road is marshy, but two-thirds of the road frontage is dry hard ground. Hmm…

I climb over the remains of the dilapidated wire fencing to investigate. There's a big tree to the left with a spring at the base. That's where the marsh comes from. There are a few dips that might be wet here and there, but otherwise, the property has a hill on the right side in the middle and it also rises in the back left to a very nice hill. I hike back to it.

Standing on the hill and looking back toward 621 changes my opinion of the property completely. The whole area spreads out in a panorama.

I can even see the old farm house on the far side of the road and down in a little hollow, surrounded by a ring of trees. Ken says an elderly recluse lives there by himself.

He warns us not to try to visit him, because the guy hates visitors and may shoot first.

This hill is where I'd build the house. Wait. We don't have time or money to build a house and a barn. What am I thinking?

I make my way back to the car and head home.

But as the search for a new property drags on, I finally mention it to Nancy.

"Wasn't it supposed to be too wet?"

I explain my new impression of the property.

"There aren't any buildings."

"We could rent a house somewhere else for now and put up a quick barn for the horses. Then I can build a house."

"That's impossible. We'd be on the road all day back and forth to the barn. And the animals need constant supervision and so do the kids. Plus anyone can drive in and rip us off. No way."

So my idea crashes and burns.

**

The date for moving looms ever closer, and we still have no place to go. Nancy offers a suggestion. What if we live on the property while we're building? What if we get a house trailer to stay in until we build a house like Jim and Nan?

It's a workable idea. I call the number on the sign. Bad news. The owners refuse to split the property in half. Good news, they're so desperate to sell that we can afford all forty acres and a trailer if we use every penny of the money from the log cabin sale.

We close the deal quickly.

I call my parents to share the good news.

They're certainly more elated than I expected.

Then my dad says, "We never told you, but we spoke with Nancy's parents. We all hated that log cabin.

I'm stunned. That came completely out of the blue. Nancy and I love our 250-year-old log cabin.

I say my goodbyes before I relate all of our plans. After dad's disconcerting comment on our first farm, I don't think they're going to like a house trailer any better. I can hear them now.

"Yes, our children have become trailer trash."

35

BUMPED UP THE BARN LADDER

We've discovered the word "unusual" is an understatement when used to describe Figgy.

Not only does he have a theme song, but it turns out that Figgy has his own job description. Taylor is the first to discover it the hard way.

I'm sitting with Nancy in the paddock of the log cabin farm as she teaches Taylor a lesson on Figgy. Taylor's slightly more advanced than Dana. Nancy is teaching her to control Figgy with her legs instead of the reins.

About midway through the lesson, I'm horrified when Figgy stops abruptly and puts his head down. Taylor rolls right over his head onto the ground. It's the first time I've witnessed someone fall off a horse. Remembering my childhood experiences on horses, it shocks me. Nancy and I rush to help her, but she's instantly on her feet.

Nancy insists Taylor stand still for a minute.

"How do you feel?"

"I'm okay."

She's a bit shaken, as I am.

Nancy has her quickly remount and resume the lesson. A few minutes later, Figgy stops and slowly rolls Taylor over his head again.

This time, Nancy's upset. I'm angry. Taylor's shocked. But Figgy is indifferent.

Suddenly, Nancy laughs. She looks like a light bulb went off in her head. She puts Taylor back up on Figgy. I don't think that's a good idea and say so. Nancy shushes me.

Nancy asks Taylor if she remembers exactly what she was doing when Figgy stopped. Taylor thinks she was squeezing with her legs to make Figgy move forward more briskly. Nancy concurs.

"Let's do a test. Do exactly the same thing and don't be surprised if Figgy stops again. If he does, let go of the reins, so you won't get pulled off."

I protest, "Taylor can get hurt." She ignores me.

I watch as Taylor bravely squeezes her legs when Nancy asks.

Figgy comes to an instant halt.

"Let go," Nancy says. Taylor does, staying safely in the saddle when Figgy puts his head down.

Nancy laughs again. "Good job. Hop off and put Figgy away. You'll be riding one of the horses from now on."

Both Taylor and I are totally bewildered.

Back in the barn, Nancy explains.

"I've seen this behavior before. When I taught riding at Madeira School, they had a big thoroughbred mare named Irish Mist. She was as big as Sharon's Bear, and she would tote beginners around safely forever. But the older instructors there told me that once the riders stopped asking her to do things and started to tell her what to do, the mare bucked them off. And I saw

Irish Mist do it again and again. I think Figgy is doing the same thing, only more carefully. Taylor, you've stopped asking Figgy to do what you want and started telling him. Figgy is telling you, in his not so subtle way, you're no longer a beginner. Starting tomorrow, you'll graduate to one of the horses. So congratulations!"

Taylor's worried expression changes to a huge smile. I enjoy the look of earned pride on her face. She makes me smile too when she gives Figgy a big hug.

So we learn that Figgy has a job description. His carries beginners safely. Nancy says he's unbelievably safe. Never a sudden move, and anything he's asked to do, he does happily and promptly. But to him, the word "beginner" is in his job title. He takes that word very seriously.

I had thought Junior was as nutty as an animal can be. It looks like Figgy is going to give her a run for her money -- er, our money.

Is it too much to hope that Figgy doesn't have any more tricks up his sleeve?

36

HOME SWEET TRAILER

I quickly get to work on our new property. We haven't closed on the log cabin farm with Vance's customers yet, but that date is coming up quickly.

I'm going to build our new barn on the back twenty-acre piece. Eventually, we'll build a house back on that hill with the great view. I have some building experience from working on our family home with my Dad, and I'm looking forward to the project. In the meantime, we'll live in a trailer near the front of the property.

While we're waiting for the log cabin farm sale to close, I need to put up two run-in sheds and add to the fencing already on two sides of the fields.

I've planned out the first run-in shed with a small field. Then another shed with a larger field that will be bigger and split up the middle. It will have an area for a small group of horses and on the other side will be space to store hay, feed, and barn paraphernalia. The cats can also call it home for the summer until the barn is built.

Those horses can live outside while I'm building the barn. They'll use the sheds to get away from bad weather or too much sun. Then there's a group of horses that need to be in stalls, which I haven't figured that out yet. One thing at a time.

The sheds go up quickly. I salvage unused telephone poles for the supports and plywood for the walls and roof. I even manage to stockpile enough extra telephone poles for building the barn. The house trailer goes in easily along with the septic field, water, and power. Jim and Nan have already moved into a house trailer on their property.

I complain about Figgy one day when I'm visiting Southern States for supplies.

Owen, the clerk who helped me with the automatic waterers, makes my day.

"What you need, Brad, is an electric fence." If I string a wire around the top of my fence and attach it to a power source, it will mildly zap any animal that touches it. Without harming them, it keeps the animals away from the fence and in the field. Why haven't I heard of this before?

I'll admit it. The thought of zapping Figgy the next time he tries to escape makes me smile. It's a good thing Nancy isn't around to hear me. I'm sure she won't think zapping is funny.

An electric fence. Perfect. No way the horses, even Figgy, can escape from that.

37

THE BALLAD OF WHIMSEY HILL

We're down to twenty-six horses. Nancy donated Ernie to the Rock Creek Mounted Police unit in Washington, D.C. Bodonis is going to be an equitation horse in Texas.

We should be at twenty-four horses.

Then Junior has her foal. It's a filly that's going to be gray when she's older and eventually white, like the stallion Nancy and Sharon chose for her father. For now, she's black with a few white hairs interspersed.

It's fun to watch her totter around like a stilt-walker on her disproportionately long legs. It was an easy birth for mother and foal and lots of fun for all the kids. Every movie with horses seems to show a foal born, but it's still not the same as the real thing.

The kids quickly bestow the foal with a name: Silver Buttons. Buttons for short.

Soon after Buttons arrives, our vet, Dr. Clark, calls out of the blue and asks us to take a pony. I explain that we're trying to cut down and can't possibly add another mouth to feed when Nancy grabs the phone.

"What's up?"

"I'm treating a small pony that shows the beginning stages of founder. The man who owns her knows nothing about ponies and his kids aren't interested. She needs a new home where someone will take care of her properly. I thought of you because the pony's a love. She'll be perfect for Lynn and Anne."

"We'll take her. If we can't use her, we'll find someone who can."

So we're back to twenty-six horses. At least the foal and the small pony won't eat much.

The pony is tiny and gray. That's white in her case, like Figgy, and about a third of his size. She does seem sweet. Let's hope she doesn't share the same hang-ups as Figgy. She's not on the property half an hour before Lynn and Anne name her Whimsey, after our farm.

That brings up something that I've been meaning to ask Nancy for ages.

"Where did the name for the farm come from?"

"When Sharon and I first started showing Junior, we noticed many of the top horses were shown under the name of a farm. We thought that sounded prestigious, so we wanted to show Junior under a farm name, too. There was a slight problem in that we didn't own a farm, but we ignored that. Finally, we came up with word whimsey --"

"-- because it's a figment of the imagination?"

"You got it. Since our farm also fit that description, we thought it was funny and a perfect choice. We added 'hill' which had a nice ring."

"Didn't it matter that there was no farm?"

"Nobody ever asked. Besides, we did own a small piece of

land."

I'm confused and say so.

"Sharon packed a bucket with dirt, planted a small juniper tree, and painted the bucket with our stable colors. Across the bottom, she lettered 'Whimsey Hill Farm.' We carried it to horse shows with us and used it for decoration outside Junior's stall. If anyone had asked, that was our piece of land, our farm, complete with tree."

I can only shake my head. I think Nancy and Sharon shared more than one figment of the imagination -- they cornered the whole market.

38

DON'T LOOK A GIFT DOG IN THE MOUTH

Nancy answers the ringing phone. It's Mrs. Hutcheson, the mother of three girls, two of whom Nancy taught riding at Madeira School. The older girls are out of school and working these days. Mrs. Hutcheson needs a favor.

I can guess from the furtive glance Nancy sends my way, I'm not going to like it.

"Lauren's dog doesn't get along with the owner's dog on the farm where she lives and works. If she can't find it a home, she'll lose her job. Can you possibly take it?"

"I guess so. If it gets along with our dog."

"There's one thing I should warn you about. Lauren bred her dog and it's expecting puppies."

"No-o-o-o!" slips out of my mouth.

**

The new dog's name is Foxy. She's a Jack Russell Terrier, a new breed to me.

About the size of a large, full grown cat. She's white with light brown patches.

I'm not sure if our residence suits her. According to her papers, she's from a royal lineage of dogs from the Duke of Beaufort's kennel in Great Britain. Let's hope she's content living in a trailer with us mere mortals when we move.

"You promise you'll have her spayed as soon as possible?"

"Yes, dear," Nancy agrees.

"We absolutely cannot keep the puppies," I reiterate.

"Don't worry. Jack Russells are popular. We shouldn't have any trouble selling them."

"You can sell them?"

"Two to three hundred apiece."

I point at Foxy, "For one of those?"

"Yes."

"How many puppies will there be?"

"Maybe four to eight."

Hmm. That's pretty nice multiplication. Finally, an animal who's going to help pay the bills.

Welcome to the funny farm, Foxy.

39

FUN AND GAMES

Nancy's expecting buyers today, so I volunteer to do the grocery shopping.

My half-acre garden is doing better this year. Unfortunately, after all the time I've spent property hunting and building, the weeds are winning again. It galls me to see tomatoes and other vegetables that I planted on the grocery shopping list.

I'm heading to the Safeway in nearby Middleburg. It's a small, pre-Civil War town in the shadow of the Blue Ridge Mountains. The area surrounding the town is comprised of large estates, farms, and an occasional vineyard.

Slightly closer to the Blue Ridge Mountains than we are, the land rolls more, although it's still dotted with rich grassy fields and woods. It's the perfect location for its main product: horses for horse sports. Many top competitive show horses, three-day event horses, dressage horses, and race horses live around Middleburg.

Nancy attends a lot of horse shows in this area.

I'm almost to the Safeway when a guy jumps in front of my car, waving frantically for traffic to stop. I brake hard. What now?

Suddenly a group of horsemen dressed in Union Army uniforms from the Civil War race by, galloping right up the main street of town. Hot on their heels is a band of Confederate horseman, whooping and hollering. One of them fires a black powder pistol in the air. Sabers rattle, hooves clatter on the street.

For a minute, I'm transported back in time.

Nancy warned me, but this is the first time I've seen it. What fun.

Re-enactments of the Civil War are big in our area. The battlefields at close by Manassas host regular events. But the Civil War was fought all over Virginia, so even a small town like Middleburg has plenty of history. Most Southerners prefer to call it the "War Between the States."

Sounds of the re-enactment fade away and I drive on.

Besides reenactments, Nancy's horsey friends are into all kinds of made up games. So far, we've been to a yard party. That's where you get a square yard of material from the host to make a costume to wear. That was a summer party, but still I wasn't happy wearing only a loin cloth.

Kentucky Derby viewing parties are yearly reoccurrences. Mint juleps are served. Betting is available. The requirement for women is large funky hats, men wear top hats. Under the hats people generally wear shorts, jeans and flip-flops. An unusual mix, but as New York fashion magazines note, Middleburg is the place where women wear barn shoes under their Dior and Balenciaga evening gowns.

There's a "Rites of Spring" party which, thank goodness, we haven't been invited to yet. I hear it includes no clothing of any sort. I leave that one to the imagination.

As I arrive at the Safeway, I remember an evening of

216

broomstick polo that we played on its parking lot after hours. There were three pairs to a team. One of each pair rode in a grocery cart and handled the broom. The other pushed the cart. I still have bruises from that one.

Once we were asked to an intimate dinner where each couple is asked to bring a special dish. Right there I should have known better. Nancy agreed to bake a cake. She decided on a tricky family favorite called a Dorothy Cake. It has a kind of light cocoa flavor. Half the time, the cake falls. It's not a pretty sight, but our family doesn't care because it still tastes good.

Unfortunately, on the day of the dinner Nancy is busy with a sick horse. She rushes into the house late and throws the cake in the oven as fast as she can. Then she heads for a quick shower. It's a given that the cake bombs.

The recipe calls for a lot of frothy frosting. Nancy decides that the frosting will hide the cake and piles it on thickly.

By the time we arrive at the dinner party, we learn something new about Dorothy Cake. The icing doesn't travel well. It slithers down to one end and the car jiggles it into a soup like texture. We're already late, so finding a store and buying a replacement isn't an option.

The dinner becomes an exercise in embarrassment.

Everyone is dressed in cocktail type clothes. We're not. The dining room table is elegantly set. Bone china, Gorham silver, immaculate white linens, Waterford crystal, and candles softly glowing from tall candelabra. It's lovely. Normally, I would love this.

The appetizers are one couple's favorite imported cheese with caviar and crackers on the side. The roast is from a steer raised by another couple. I get flashes of Pork Chop and my weed filled garden when I hear this.

Specially raised green beans and potatoes are the side dishes with peaches from a home orchard. These people are successfully self-sufficient in a way that I envy.

And then, when the exquisite dinner ends, our cake is served.

Everyone's polite, but we aren't asked back. Ever.

Did I mention Nancy can't cook?

When I return to the log cabin farm with groceries, I get out to open the gate. I can see the sawdust truck has come and gone, leaving a huge pile of sawdust in front of the barn. Nancy uses it for bedding in the stalls. I'll have to get a tarp over it as soon as possible to protect it from rain and dew.

Actually, I'm kind of surprised to see the new sawdust. Last time the sawdust driver was here, it didn't end well.

The driver and Nancy got in a heated argument when the driver tried to raise the bill over the agreed price. Nancy didn't want me to get involved. Shakey had no such inhibitions.

As the argument went on, Shakey strolled around behind the driver. When he was directly behind him, Shakey lifted his leg against the driver's pants and peed.

The disagreement ended immediately. The driver, cursing and complaining, grabbed the pre-written check from Nancy, jumped in his truck, and left.

Shakey flashed his grin at Nancy and then at me. I swear the dog has a sense of humor. I snickered for the rest of the day. What a good dog.

I drive the car through the gate and get out to close it. Wait. Shakey's suddenly climbing up the sawdust pile. What's he doing? I hope he's not going to make a mess and spread it around.

By the time I close the gate, Junior's foal, Buttons, has joined

Shakey at the pile.

The two of them are face to face with their noses only about a foot apart. Junior grazes unconcerned nearby, but I'm anxious that the two animals might hurt each other. I don't see Nancy anywhere around.

I leave the car and hurry toward the barn to shoo them away from each other.

All of a sudden, Shakey and Buttons start bouncing around. Right to left, left to right. Like mirror images. Shakey breaks away and races up the sawdust pile and back down. He no sooner hits the ground, then Buttons darts up the pile and down again.

Then Shakey repeats the dash up and down. Buttons heads to the top again, but this time she stops on the top.

I stop, too, trying to figure out what's going on. Why isn't Junior upset that the dog is harassing her foal?

Shakey charges up the pile, confronts the foal, who doesn't move, and runs down again.

A second later, Shakey's in possession of the top and the foal slides to the bottom. Sawdust flies everywhere.

But I don't interfere. I figured it out. They're playing King of the Hill. I can't believe it. They're making a huge mess but it doesn't matter; I'll rake it up when they're done.

A dog and a foal. Neither is trying to hurt the other. I wouldn't have believed it.

They're just having fun.

First, tag with Junior, now Shakey and Buttons. Who knew that animals played games too?

I lean back against the car to watch the fun.

40

BRAD BE NIMBLE, BRAD BE QUICK

I should have listened to the people who said our new property is marshy. It rained for the last two days. There's mud everywhere. Junior must think she's in Heaven. Not me.

There's a rutted dirt track which goes from the center of the road frontage of the property to the middle, then peters out. I'm going to use it as the main driveway to the barn I will build. The only things back there now are the new sheds and fields.

I drove down it today, exactly like I have every other time. I get about a hundred feet past the geographical center of the property when the pick-up truck sinks like a rock. Great.

No way it's moving. I hop out to look at the damage.

Bad idea. My boots disappear into the mud. I cling to the side of the truck to stay upright. When I take a step, the mud sucks one of my short slip-on boots right off my foot. With my socked foot dangling in the air, I watch in horror as the mud closes over my boot.

I also realize there's no way to move without putting my foot back down into the mud. I could scramble into the back of the pickup, but that would only be temporary. Unless I plan to take up residence in the truck bed, sooner or later, I'll have to cross the mud to reach solid ground.

In a moment of total lunacy, I tell myself, "If I run fast enough, I can stay on top of the mud." Before I'm smart enough to rethink the idea, I put it into action, launching myself in the direction of dry ground.

Reality strikes as my first foot sinks. Now I'm flat on my face in the mud. As an engineer, I should have known better. Moving quicker only succeeds in driving my foot in deeper. I guess running faster to cross things that can't support you only works in "Roadrunner" cartoons.

As I lie here a question floats through my mind.

This life, where I spend a lot of time flat on my face in the mud -- is it working?

By the time I crawl to dry ground, I've lost my sock, too.

I look back at the tires. The mud's up to the axles.

Just how muddy is this property?

It's only a couple weeks until I move Nancy and the kids into the house trailer.

The log cabin farm settlement has been postponed a month. I'm trying to use every extra minute to prep the new property.

The sheds and electric fences are in.

I can't afford to lose time dealing with the truck, much less the mud. Luckily, I know Jim is working over on his property. I limp and squish the half mile up to his place.

After a quick change into some borrowed clothes and boots, he drives me back with his pickup. We hook my pickup to his with a chain he carries. I can tell I'll have to get one.

It takes a while, but the pickup grudgingly comes out. As for my boot, it has totally disappeared.

Nancy's unsympathetic response to my tale of woe is, "Did I think my lost boot would grow little boots in the spring?"

I'm not amused, but I manage, "Yes, but they'll only be left ones."

"Then you better go back and plant the other one so we'll have a pair of shoe trees."

Our humor has hit a new low.

**

Sadly, Clarence passes away unexpectedly one night right before we move. His health hasn't been good for a while, but it is still a shock. Maybe it was a good thing we were moving because the log cabin farm doesn't feel the same without him.

I remember how he used to con Sharon into reading the sports pages to him. He would claim he couldn't find his glasses and the print was too small. Only none of us ever saw him wearing glasses. We guessed that he might not be able to read.

Sharon never minded. The two of them would sit in front of the barn and work their way through the paper, eating the corn bread that Sharon's mother baked especially for him.

One of my favorite memories of Clarence is last Christmas Eve after Anne and Lynn had gone to bed. He had purchased a red Radio Flyer wagon for the kids. It was way too expensive a gift on the money he earned as a groom, but he insisted.

It came unassembled. So he and I sat on the floor in the kitchen and put it together while Nancy wrapped the remaining presents. Somehow the directions had been lost for the wagon, but we had fun trying to figure out what went where. It was a warm, special evening. I remember the look of pride on his face when he placed the finished wagon under the Christmas tree. And his even bigger look of pride on Christmas day when the wagon turned out to be a smash hit with Lynn and Anne.

41

NO CONTINGENCY HAS A CONTINGENCY

The move into the trailer goes well with one exception. The thirty-five ton well drilling rig sinks into the mud. Not too uncommon a problem for well drilling rigs, so they come with jacks to pull themselves out. Unfortunately, that doesn't work. Nor does a bulldozer. Eventually, we create a path of rocks under and in front of it for the rig to gain some traction. Then with the aid of the bulldozer, it comes free.

As usual, Nancy has her own solution to the mud spots. She goes to a close out sale at a local gardening nursery. There she buys two four-foot-tall willow trees. The trunks are about the size of a thumb.

The cost? A dollar each. She plants one in the spot where our pickup sank and one where the well drilling rig sank.

I don't get it and I say so.

"Willow trees are water seekers and grow fast. They'll be happy in a mud hole, keep vehicles out of that area, and dry the spots out." I'm not convinced, but I've learned to wait and see. Some of her weird ideas actually do work.

**

Anyone who makes disparaging remarks about house trailers has never been in one.

The second-hand, single wide trailer Nancy and I selected in West Virginia for the farm isn't a high end model, yet it contains three bedrooms, two full bathrooms, space for a dining table, a kitchen, and an expanded living room. The wall colors, shag rugs, and faux wood paneling leave a bit to be desired, but the trailer definitely serves our purpose. Still, as we expected, our parents aren't any more thrilled with our trailer living than they were with us in our log cabin.

So now there are the four of us, the twins, Shakey, and Foxy. Lynn and Anne share the bedroom on one end. The twins have bunk beds in the middle bedroom.

Nancy and I have the bedroom on the other end. Even with such a big trailer, there are times it feels very crowded. Especially when Wood is charging from one end of the trailer to the other, having a Wood fit.

The farm next door to the new property is owned by an elderly couple who no longer farm. They have a vacant barn and offer it to us at no cost. What kind people they are and what an unexpectedly lucky solution.

Nancy manages to get us down to ten horses before the move. She had to cut the prices to bone to do it, but it really helped our situation. Figgy, Whimsey, Junior, a racetrack reject named Sailor's Legend and nicknamed Morris, and six other skinny track rejects that need fattening up. Only two will live in the neighbors' barn.

And that's when we get the really bad news.

Vance, the real estate agent, calls.

The sale of the log cabin farm has fallen through.

"How can that be? We have a no contingency contract."

According to Vance, "The state of Virginia rules a contract null and void automatically if a buyer can't qualify for financing."

Our lawyer confirms this. It would have been nice if we were warned of the possibility up front. So even a no contingency contract has a contingency.

Great. There's no way I can carry two properties financially.

After an anxious discussion, it's clear that the log cabin farm will go on the market. It's a popular size of property and has a house and barn. It should sell faster than a marshy property with no buildings.

Of course, all those real estate agents that bugged us constantly about selling it have disappeared. Even Vance has gone. I'm now paying six mortgages on my meager salary. A first and second mortgage, plus some cash to Nancy's parents, for the purchase of the log cabin farm, plus a first, second, and third loan on the new property that we took out to bridge the gap until the money from the sale of the log cabin farm comes through.

This is a total catastrophe.

All construction on the new property comes to an immediate halt.

42

ROUND 'EM UP

I arrive home from my business trip to California to some good news.

Figgy is in.

Did I mention I love electric fencing? At least one good thing has come from our move to the trailer.

I manage to wait until after dinner to break my news to Nancy.

"I've heard of a position I really want."

"In California?"

"No, only about thirteen miles further into Maryland than where I am now." I can see the relief in her face even though she tries to mask it.

"I met a man who's at the National Bureau of Standards in Gaithersburg. He's one of the top men in my field. He has these dynamic new plans for robotics. And he wants my machine tool expertise. Can you imagine? I'll be the fourth man hired for his team. I'll be able to design original hardware and do all kinds of new things."

She smiles at my excitement.

"There is one big drawback..."

The smile fades.

"It involves international travel. The trips will be longer. Would you mind?"

The smile returns. "It sounds exciting. You should go for it."

I send my resume the next morning.

**

Shakey's changed since we moved to the new property. He's become very territorial. He seems to know exactly where the property lines are even though I've never even walked them with him.

Twice I've seen strange dogs cut through our land. Shakey runs at them full tilt, hitting them in their sides, and bowling them over like an NFL linebacker. By the time they get back on their feet, they run as fast as they can to get off our property. Shakey doesn't bark or bite them, he just bowls them over. Even a huge German Shepherd couldn't leave fast enough. No dogs Shakey knocked over have made a return visit.

I was telling Nancy about Shakey's territorial behavior at breakfast after I returned from California.

Lynn interrupts, "Daddy, cows in the yard."

It can't be. We don't have one anymore.

I race to the front door of the trailer and look out.

There are six brown cattle grazing on our front yard.

Nancy comes up behind me. "They belong to that huge farm across the street. Somebody leases the pastures there."

At that second, Shakey squeezes past my legs and out the door.

"Call him back. Quick. He'll scatter them."

230

I race for my shoes.

When I return to the door, Nancy's quiet.

"Why aren't you calling him?"

"Look."

There's Shakey, collecting the cattle quietly in a group. Like he's herded cattle all his life, he heads them across the road.

We can see from the trailer that the gate to their field is hanging on its hinges.

Shakey directs them through the gate and comes back. I've never seen anything like it. Nancy's as amazed as I am.

How does he know how to do that? He grew up in a suburb. How did he know where to take them? He's never done that with any of our animals.

I grab a hammer and some nails and race over to the gate to put it back together before the cattle can get out again.

I stop on the way to praise Shakey. He saved me a lot of time. So help me, I swear he grins at me.

I ask Nancy if she's ever seen him do that.

"Of course. It is a smile. He's very expressive. Haven't you noticed? He's got a sense of humor like Junior."

"So he deliberately peed on the sawdust truck driver?"

"He was showing his contempt the only way he could. Either that or he smelled another dog on the driver's pants and was staking out his territory."

Hmm. I not sure I buy that dogs smile, but I sure hope Shakey never gets mad at me.

43

SHORTCUT TO HAPPINESS

I get the new job. It's like being paid to play every day. How lucky is that?

The tiny increase in pay is also welcome. Not enough to pay off any mortgages, but every penny helps. There's a major downside, though. The extra thirteen miles makes my total commute an hour and fifteen minutes each way.

It means I'm home that much less. I knew there'd be some increase in the commute, but I didn't expect it to feel so much longer. Nancy hasn't said anything about it yet, but if I combine the added time on the road with the upcoming international travel, I realize I'm dropping a lot into Nancy's hands, which are already full.

My lab at the Bureau of Standards isn't that far the way the crow flies. But the Potomac River divides the farm from my job. There's one bridge on the Washington Beltway, miles to the south of the farm. So I have to go south for the heavily used bridge, cross the bridge, and then turn north again in heavy traffic to get to Gaithersburg. My other option is to go north to the lesser used, but still distant, Route 15 bridge at Point of Rocks, then turn south on the other side of the river.

Ken listens patiently as I complain while on a gas and snack expedition with Lynn, Anne, and the twins.

"Have you ever taken the ferry?"

"What?"

"White's Ferry." He can tell I don't know what he's talking about.

"It's about a third of the way to Point of Rocks from Leesburg. Could save you a bunch of time." Ken gives me directions.

A ferry in the middle of the rural countryside. Who knew?

I turn to the girls.

"Grab your drinks ladies. We're going to find a ferry." And find it we do. Route 15 from Leesburg to Point of Rocks is farm country on both sides. I pass the tiny road between two fields just outside Leesburg twice before I spot the miniscule, one-foot by six-inch weathered sign that says White's Ferry. The narrow road looks like the driveway to a farmhouse. First it goes between the fields, then it dips down through thick trees.

I turn into the road with trepidation. It doesn't look like an area that gets any commercial traffic. Not a building in sight.

Lynn and Anne pepper me with questions. What's a ferry? Where does it go? What's it for?

I answer as best I can. I notice the twins listening, too.

When I reach the tree line, the road takes a sharp left, and the dip becomes steeper. Now we can actually see the river. I had no idea we were so close to it. We go a few hundred feet further and there's a little park on the river bank and a loading area for the ferry.

234

I pull the car over into the park and stop. I want to check out the ferry. The girls finish their snacks as we watch.

The ferry, named the General Jubal A. Early, after a Confederate Civil War General, if I remember right, is a flat barge. Twenty or so cars can drive right on and off.

The Potomac is narrow here, maybe a thousand feet wide. A cable stretches across the river and the ferry is attached to it. The ferry motors back and forth by sliding along the cable.

The only buildings in sight are on the far side. One is a stone building which has a sandwich and coffee shop on the bottom level and what seems like living quarters above. It looks about two and a half stories. The other seems to be a home. It looks like you can rent canoes and skiffs, too.

We feed the snack remains to a group of wild ducks at the water's edge. Then I round up the girls.

"Let's go for a ferry ride." I can tell they've been watching it, too. They excitedly pile back in the car.

Once out on the water in the ferry, there's a beautiful view up and down the river. It's all trees along the banks, predominantly willows and oaks. Still no buildings in sight except the two where the ferry docks. It's easy to imagine what the river was like a hundred years ago. Very cool.

I'm pleased to see all four girls enjoying it, too.

Once the cars are loaded onto the ferry, the trip takes about fifteen minutes. One of the ferrymen mentions there are old pictures in the sandwich shop.

When we get out on the Maryland side, I stop again in another small park area.

Through signs there, we discover that the Chesapeake & Ohio Canal which used to run parallel to the Potomac from

235

Washington, D.C. to Cumberland, Maryland passed right here. The signs say coal from the Allegheny Mountains was the primary cargo.

Here and there in the park are a few remaining sections of the canal's banks.

The biggest remnant is an old metal bridge that used to cross it.

We head across the street to the main ferry building. Inside we find a local store like Ken's, with walls full of old memorabilia, including interesting pictures of the ferry and the canal.

We discover that there used to be more than a hundred ferries in the surrounding area crossing the Potomac. Of all those, only White's Ferry is left. We also learn that almost this entire building was underwater during Hurricane Agnes, when we nearly lost Izzy and Dana.

"It was a once in a hundred years' event," the store proprietor tells us as he points to a mark on the outside front of the store.

I judge the building is about six to eight feet above the current river level and the mark on the building showing where the flood water reached is an additional twenty feet. That would make the river during Agnes approximately twenty-seven feet higher than it is now. When you add in the width of the flatter Maryland side, the pure volume of water flowing through here must have been staggering.

I notice Dana has gone quiet.

I mentally give thanks for Izzy's and Dana's survival that night and hustle the girls to the car to change the subject.

**

When we arrive back home, before I can even tell Nancy about my great new shortcut to work and how I can save twenty minutes of driving, she interrupts me.

"Foxy had her puppies."

44

CAMP WHIMSEY HILL

Foxy has seven puppies. It's fun watching them. I build an open box for them, line the bottom with newspaper, and then add a layer of wood shavings. We place it in the corner of our room to give Foxy a quiet spot.

I watch as Nancy carefully instructs Lynn and Anne how to approach Foxy and the puppies quietly. She has them sit near the box. Then she lifts a puppy and puts one in each girl's lap. She also tells them about being careful the puppies don't get smothered.

The puppies soon acquire names: Tommy, Snuggles, Jane Russell, Rusty, Rustler, Widdle, and Kurt Russell. They're all white with different colored spots. They become the center of attraction in our house.

**

Since all work on the property involving money is on hold until we sell the log cabin farm, I use the time to cut the telephone poles I stockpiled to the lengths I'll need for the new barn's vertical posts. Using a borrowed chainsaw is a little scary, but I get the hang of it quickly.

Once I get them cut, I plan to lay out the barn and begin sinking the poles, digging each of the holes by hand. It's a job that moves the barn building forward. I also manage to plant some potatoes behind the trailer. Whenever we can, Jim and I go back and forth to help each other with any two-man jobs.

**

I have to admit, the puppies are cute. They've been with us about nine weeks when I start asking, "Isn't it about time to sell them?" I quickly incur dirty looks from my family and the twins.

Taylor and Dana have begun creating songs about their experiences with us on the farm.

One of them starts like this: "The horses here at Whimsey They say they're mighty fine.

One has three legs, one has two, But the one with one is mine.

The popcorn here at Whimsey, They say it's mighty fine.

Some fell to the floor, And killed a dog of mine."

Yup, that's us. Morbid Camp Whimsey. The verses only get worse from here.

**

One cold, rainy winter evening, when Izzy and the twins are staying over, I hear Nancy tell Taylor that we need potatoes for dinner. It makes me smile.

I'm a highly educated, well-traveled individual. But seeing my potatoes served for our family meals gives me a great kick.

Taylor tells Izzy it's her turn, and that the pitchfork is outside the back door.

Izzy hasn't been overnight since the potatoes were ready to harvest so she doesn't know the drill.

Izzy's response from the warm couch in front of the TV is,

240

"So?"

"Potatoes." Comes again from the kitchen.

Taylor explains to Izzy, "We need one potato for each of us."

Izzy dutifully heads out into the cold rain to dig, and Taylor and Dana set the table. When Izzy returns with the potatoes, she's freezing and soaked to the skin. She passes the potatoes into the kitchen and heads into the bathroom to get out of her wet clothes and into pajamas.

Later that evening, when the twins prep for bed, Taylor and Dana discover that Izzy's wet clothes are spread all over their shared bathroom, drenching everything.

In the morning, Izzy can't find her jeans. I catch the smirk on Taylor's and Dana's faces as Izzy worriedly searches.

I recognize the signs. I was a pretty big practical joker in school, so I enjoy the kids going at it as long as it doesn't go too far.

Eventually, Izzy finds her jeans outside the back door. They're frozen solid. So much so, they can stand up on their own.

Annoyed by the bathroom mess, Taylor and Dana had waited for her to go to bed and then hung her jeans outside.

**

In spite of the negative responses, I keep asking. "When do the puppies go?"

They're tumbling all over our bedroom floor now.

Nancy makes a few calls to let people know we have puppies for sale. I'm still amazed at the prices they could bring. Nancy tells me Jack Russells aren't even a registered breed of dog with the American Kennel Club. I guess they're really popular with horse people.

"There's a slight change of plans," Nancy says.

241

I hope I didn't hear her right.

"Lynn and Anne are very attached to Snuggles and Tommy. I think we should keep those two. I believe a child should grow up with a dog if possible."

"Aren't Shakey and Foxy dogs?"

"Shakey is a family dog. Foxy hasn't attached herself to Lynn or Anne. I'm talking about a dog that's special to each child."

"We don't need four dogs."

"Well, three actually. An acquaintance in Warrenton who's a friend of the people who own the puppies' father has asked for Foxy. She has a huge farm and loves dogs. She fell in love with Foxy when she saw her."

I remember the kids' faces while they're holding Snuggles and Tommy. Call me a pushover. At least the puppies have somewhat normal names. I couldn't face another named Mary, Mother of God.

Three dogs it is. At least it's better than nine.

Nancy and I break the news to Lynn and Anne. The joy on their faces is worth every penny I know it's going to cost me.

45

HAYMAKER

Coming home from work, I turn into our driveway and accidentally block Curtis' pickup as he's backing out. I haven't seen him in awhile. I wonder how his mother is.

I pull aside to let him pass.

In the back of the property, I can see Nancy mowing the grass with the bush hog. A bush hog is a heavy duty mower that is dragged behind a tractor. They mow fields and are great for rough and overgrown areas. In Virginia the spring rain, summer humidity, and thunderstorms make things grow thick and fast.

"Hi, Curtis. What's up?" I notice he seems nervous, almost uncomfortable.

"I wanted to ask you about cuttin' your hay this year. I had a deal with the old owners."

"What hay?" Why do people keep giving me that look like I'm stupid.

"Your entire property is timothy."

"Isn't that the kind of hay that horses eat?" Apparently it is. I can tell because I get the look again.

Our entire property is timothy? I just thought it was grass. Maybe I am that stupid.

"What did Nancy say?"

"I didn't...she's busy. Thought I'd come by again when you was here."

I glance at Nancy again. I smile. She's mowing, but she's also sunbathing in her bikini so she can get a tan.

Curtis is definitely embarrassed. I wonder if he's ever seen a woman in a bathing suit. My money's on not.

I can't resist paying Curtis back for "the look."

"Let's drive back and see what she says."

He can't quite hide his alarm.

"Umm...I...why don't I just talk to you?"

I relent. "So what's the deal?"

"I make the hay and give you a third."

"That's baled and fit for horses?"

He nods.

"Make it half. Deal?"

"Deal."

Timothy. Who knew?

**

The next day, I stop by our local Farm Agent in Leesburg. The U.S. Department of Agriculture has an office and an agent in most farm counties in the U.S. They offer free farming advice on everything from barn building to planting corn. They're also there to answer specific questions from farmers and newbies like me.

The agent gives me the rundown on timothy hay. When he's answered all my questions, he has one of his own.

"Have you visited the county tax office?"

I haven't. "Should I?"

244

"If you sell some of that hay, you may qualify for a reduction in real estate taxes."

Ten minutes later, after some misdirection, I'm at the counter in the tax office with a tiny, wrinkled woman clerk who must be a hundred and ten years old. She runs me through the tax reduction questions.

"Do you have more than ten acres?"

Check.

"Do you produce livestock or produce?"

"We have a steer."

"Personal use?"

"What does that mean?"

"To sell?"

"No."

She shakes her head.

"Do horses and hay count?" They do! Thank you, Buttons. She counts as raising livestock, and timothy.

Check.

"How much income do they produce a year?" Income? Oops.

"That's necessary?"

Apparently it is.

"Can I get back to you on that?" She gives me all the forms to fill out and mail in.

At home I go over the tax papers carefully. If we make around seven hundred dollars a year from the farm, we qualify for the reduced real estate taxes. I'll have to count how many bales come off our property this year. Nancy agrees to keep track of what our horses eat on average. If the difference is enough to make the qualifying tax amount, we'll be making hay next year, literally.

Finally, there's a way to make this farm earn some money. Timothy isn't the same as a garden, but it is a crop.

46

FIGGY BY MOONLIGHT

It's late. 2a.m. at least. But sleep doesn't come. It's often like this when Nancy's away overnight.

She says it's the same for her when I'm on a business trip. Anne and Lynn sleep in their room. Dana occupies one of the bunk beds in the middle bedroom.

Taylor's away with Nancy at a show.

I relax and listen to the night noises. The big barn owl the twins saw the other evening hoots softly. I imagine him soaring in the full moon. The moonlight must make his evening hunt easier.

At least he's not scary like the screech owl we had at the log cabin farm. When he hooted, if you call it that, he'd raise you straight up out of bed.

The other nighttime "bed raiser" we had at the log cabin was some kind of bobcat that passed through maybe once a year. You could hear him coming in the distance, pass close by, and then disappear into the opposite distance, howling all the way. I'm not sure what the howling was about. We conjectured that it meant, "get out of my way."

I hear a scraping sound from the driveway. And there it is again. What can that be?

Concerned, I head for a window.

I recognize that white blur. It's Figgy. He's heading down the driveway toward Route 621.

I glance around. The only shoes quickly available are Nancy's fluffy, neon green slippers. I shove my feet into them and slip out the back door. I immediately feel the chilly evening air on my bare chest. Luckily, I have my pajama bottoms on.

The moonlight makes for good visibility.

Figgy munches grass along the side of the driveway. When he spots me, he takes off, stopping right where the driveway joins the road.

Desperate, I pick grass and try the same old trick, pretending I have food.

"Hi, Figgy. It's just me. You know me. Look I have some nice, yummy grass.

Figgy's not buying my message. Why does it always work for Nancy? I've seen her throw gravel in a bucket and the horses come to her. Does she make the non-food sound better tasting than I do?

I attempt to get in front of him to block him from the road. Unfortunately the driveway is too narrow as it goes through the open gate posts.

Figgy doesn't like my coming so close. He moves onto the road.

Rats. Good thing it's late and there's no traffic. I don't know if I'm helping or hurting at this point. Figgy drops his head to graze on the road's edge and I manage to ease around him without spooking him.

248

I walk back toward him, holding the grass out and talking to him. I must be getting better at it because this time I manage to walk right up to him.

I feed him my handful of grass. His muzzle hair tickles my palm. I reach down slowly, pull some more grass and give it to him. This time I pet him on the neck. He stands still and lets me.

It's then I realize I have a problem.

He has no halter on.

I have no way to control him.

I give him a shove back toward our gate. He doesn't budge an inch. This isn't good.

If I only had a scarf, a rope, or anything that I could wrap around his neck, I could lead him. I see Nancy and the twins lead horses that way for short distances all the time. There must be something. A good strong vine? No. I'd have to leave Figgy to find one and I don't know if he'd let me get this close again. Besides, if I pull a vine out of the fence, it may make noise and frighten him off.

I shiver...and get an idea.

It's only a hundred feet back to the driveway. There's not a car in sight. Once I'm in the driveway, no one will see me.

I slip out of my pajama bottoms. Easing up to Figgy, I wrap one pajama leg around his neck. This makes a loop with the other leg. When I tug on the make-shift rope, Figgy follows along perfectly.

Problem solved.

Suddenly a car's headlights blaze around the curve behind us.

Spooked, Figgy takes off. He drags me a few feet. Then his shoulder bumps me and I fall flat on my face.

Figgy continues on, my pajamas flapping around his neck. I

watch with relief as he turns in at our driveway.

The car, a beat up Chevy at least a decade old, stops beside me as I pick myself up.

A flashlight shines right in my face.

"Lookee what we've got here, partner. A naked man out for a moonlight stroll," the driver jeers.

"There was a pony..."

"-- Didn't see no pony. If you're comparin' yourself with a stallion, I'm not seein' it." They laugh hysterically.

They're totally drunk. Talking is useless. Besides, I'm getting flashes of the recent movie, *Deliverance*.

Partner pipes in, "Nice slippers, mister." I stand and, with all the aplomb I can muster, turn and head back toward our place.

The car keeps pace with me all the way. Partner and the driver use their flashlight beam as a spotlight, highlighting my various body parts.

I'm shivering and not just from the cold.

They keep up a running, unflattering commentary of my anatomy all the way.

It's the longest distance I've ever walked.

With a feeling of relief, I turn my back to them and head into our driveway.

With a honk, the car disappears down the road.

Drat you, Figgy. This is the most humiliating experience of my life. It's even worse than being locked in the tack room.

47

DRENCHED AND ANNOYED

Nancy and Taylor come home the day after my late night stroll with Figgy. She brings good news. The young horse she took to the show is sold to a student of a friend and she has people coming to see the puppies.

At the following breakfast, I tell her about Figgy's escape from the electric fence, leaving out the embarrassing parts. I lie to myself that I don't mention it because young ladies are present.

"Was the fence on?"

That never occurred to me. When we work on the fencing and during thunderstorms we turn the power off. As the horses have all been introduced to the fence and are afraid of it, there seems to be no need to leave it on all the time.

"It shouldn't have made any difference. I checked it and didn't see anywhere it was down," I say.

After we eat, I help Nancy fill the tub we have on the back of the tractor with water for the horses. I haven't installed plumbing yet at the barn site or the fenced fields with sheds.

Nancy drives the tractor out with fresh water every morning.

Since I'm headed out to dig more holes for the telephone poles, I hitch a ride with her by standing on the small running board. Shakey and Foxy run along beside us.

As we near the middle of the property, with the barn site and fenced fields coming up on our right, and the hill where I'd like to put our house eventually on the left, Nancy says, "Look."

There are three Virginia white-tailed deer grazing on top of the hill. Beautiful.

"Keep watching," she says.

As we get closer, Shakey and Foxy notice the deer still several acres away. They bark furiously and charge in the deer's direction. The deer's heads come up. They register alarm and head toward the woods in back.

The two dogs suddenly quit barking and come to a stop after only going a short distance toward the deer. Then I notice the deer have also stopped. They walk back to where they were and start grazing again. The two dogs rejoin us and continue their run beside the tractor and back to the barn area.

"What just happened? I expected the dogs to disappear over the hill in hot pursuit of the deer."

"They did that the first morning I brought the water out. Since then, this is their regular morning routine. The dogs tell the deer they're here and in charge. The deer pretend they're afraid. Then everyone goes back to whatever they were doing. It's fun to watch them."

"They do this every morning?"

"Whenever the deer are here."

**

Later that afternoon, Nancy asks for help over at the neighbor's barn with her horse named Morris. He has a cough and

252

the vet wants her to give him some medicine called a drench. Nancy explains that a drench is any liquid medicine that you pour down a horse's throat. Most horses aren't fond of this process.

Because Morris is such a big horse Nancy has to stand on a ladder to get his head up high enough to make him swallow. My job will be trying to hold him still. Not something I'm either good at or like to do.

Before we start, she tells me to watch out.

"Morris likes to tromp on people's feet."

"Likes to?"

"He does it deliberately. Be careful."

I've learned better than to say that's impossible. I've also learned that if Nancy says something about the animals, no matter how farfetched, I better listen.

We back Morris into a corner of his stall, and Nancy climbs the step ladder with the twelve-ounce plastic bottle of syrupy liquid from Dr. Clark.

Morris seems to know what's coming and isn't happy about it. He throws his head back and forth. I'm hanging on to his halter with a death grip, so he's tossing me too every time he lifts his head. Nancy finally gets him in the right position with his head up and pours the liquid down his throat. Or so she thinks.

Seconds later, Morris spits the medicine out-all over me.

He must have added a little liquid of his own, because it seems like I'm wearing more than twelve ounces. The sticky liquid totally soaks me from head to foot.

With all the aplomb I can muster, I turn to Nancy. "You forgot to mention the part about who gets drenched."

She's still laughing when Morris stomps on my foot.

"Owwwwwwww!"

I saw him sidle over beside me. I swear it was no accident. My foot hurts so much that it pisses me off.

"Anytime you want help giving Morris medicine, I'm your man," I tell Nancy.

It will give me great pleasure to hold him so Nancy can dump medicine down his throat.

"So what is he getting this for?"

"He's allergic to the timothy hay." A horse has hay fever?

"Then what does he eat?"

"He gets alfalfa."

∗∗

I take my time in the bathtub. The hot water feels good on my sore foot. It takes two doses of shampoo before my hair feels clean again. My clothes are so sticky from Morris' drench that putting them in the washing machine isn't an option. When I'm done washing, I drain the tub, and refill it to soak my clothes. Hopefully I can cut down the amount of crud before I toss them in the washing machine.

Sometimes I ask myself, "Do I have a target on my back that only animals can see?"

But apparently Morris is an equal opportunity foot stomper. I hear Taylor and Dana warn Izzy to be careful around him. Minutes later, Izzy shrieks as Morris tramples her foot.

It's a good thing Nancy insists on real footwear in the barn. Even so, I'm amazed there haven't been any broken toes yet. At this rate, it's only a matter of time. I better check our liability insurance. I know it doesn't cover acts of God. Hopefully it does cover acts of Morris.

∗∗

Lynn, almost six, and Anne, four and three quarters, are

attending their first horse show where they'll ride. Lynn in the walk-trot class on the pony, Whimsey, and Anne in the lead line on Figgy. Dana will have a class or two on Figgy. I'm taking my camera.

The weather's beautiful. Sunny and seventy. The show is a popular local one at Nokesville, Virginia.

Anne goes first in the lead line class with Nancy doing the leading. Lead line classes are fun because all the kids get ribbons and, in this case, huge pinwheel lollypops. When Anne exits the ring, she comes to find me, hiding her lollypop behind her back. Nancy follows with Figgy.

"Daddy, Daddy, guess what I won!"

"Was it an airplane?"

"No, Daddy. You're silly." She whips out her lollypop.

Only there's a problem. Instead of a flat, circular lollypop, it's crescent shaped.

There's a pony sized bite missing. We all look to Figgy. He's munching contentedly.

I'm expecting tears from Anne.

Wrong.

"It's okay, Dad. It was the two of us who won it."

I love my kids. They make me very proud.

Next Lynn is in the saddle and heads into the ring on Whimsey.

One of Nancy's professional riding friends has a son about the same age in the walk-trot class, too. The two women stand together by the rail to watch.

I have Anne up on my shoulders and am shooting pictures of Lynn, when I see a more the interesting event going on outside the ring. Nancy and her friend are nervously clutching each other while they watch their kids.

"Look out, that brown pony kicks."

"Be careful you don't get boxed in."

"That's right. Trot right out."

"Watch out for that bay pony. Stay away from him."

I've never seen Nancy like this. And the friend? She's a big time professional rider who's known for her cool. They're acting like the world's worst stage mothers.

Not what I ever expected, and it totally cracks me up.

Later, I'm sitting in the stands with Lynn and Anne, eating our picnic lunch.

Dana's class on Figgy is coming up in a little bit. I notice Lynn and Anne appear very comfortable in the horse show environment. Even though they're so young, they've been to shows with Nancy since they were born. People greet them and stop to say a few words when they pass. I'm the one they don't recognize.

Joan Wilkins, a petite woman who bought a horse for her daughter from us two years ago, slides into the seat beside us. At least she knows me. After exchanging greetings, she tells us her daughter is riding a new horse in the next class. This will be his first time to a show.

Even though her daughter's main interest is combined training events, she's brought her new horse to give him some experience with people and all the distractions that go on when they're competing.

Combined training is a different equine competition than horse shows. It includes three phases -- dressage, jumping cross country, and stadium jumping. At the top levels, it takes place over several days. Combined training was begun originally as a test for military horses, hence its inclusion in the Olympics. The dressage phase is to show obedience. The cross country phase, jumping all obstacles in its way, demonstrates the ability to help the rider escape or to get a message through. The last phase, stadium jumping, is to show endurance. Does the horse still have enough energy left after a day of cross country to still be useful? Now it's considered a test for an all-around horse. At least that's the way I understand it.

Joan says, "I don't like my daughter's new horse."

That comes out of the blue.

"Why not?"

"He scares me."

Not good.

"Whenever I'm in his stall, he tries to step on my feet."

That sounds eerily familiar.

"We have one that does that, too. I wonder if they're related?" I ask jokingly.

"Our horse is by Sailor. That's a stallion that stands over near Warrenton."

"Sailor? Why does that sound familiar?"

"Morris," says Lynn. "Sailor's Legend."

I completely forgot. Morris' real name on his papers is Sailor's Legend. Is that even possible? A genetic predisposition to stepping on peoples' feet?

**

The day has one more surprise. Of course it's Figgy.

Dana rides Figgy in the first jumping class. The jumps are low for new riders.

As with most jumping courses, there are eight jumps laid out in a pattern in the ring.

257

The surprise is that Figgy counts to eight.

Dana enters the ring, makes a small circle to get up to speed and approaches the first jump. She negotiates the course and after the eight jumps, Figgy knows the job is done and starts the circle to slow down before Dana asks him. He catches her off guard.

She tries to get him to canter further, but he slows to a walk. He's done. And he does the same thing in the next class even though the pattern of jumps is different. Eight jumps make up the typical pony hunter course.

"Counting isn't good," Nancy worries.

"He counts?" I have to ask.

"He's told us today he counts to eight, and then he figures he's done. That means he isn't listening to the kids."

Now there's a shock.

"But what will he do when there are more jumps?" We get the answer to that question pretty quickly. The course for Dana's next equitation class has ten jumps. Figgy slows again after eight. She urges him forward and he does reluctantly jump the ninth fence, but at a much slower pace. And that's it. He stops. No amount of urging from Dana can get him to continue on to the tenth jump.

She's excused from the class. That's fine with Dana.

"He's definitely counting," Nancy says. "I don't think we'll use him for jumping classes in the future."

Dana likes the flat classes better, anyway and says so.

At this point, Lynn and Anne are getting tired. It's been a long day for them. I decide to take them home for their naps. Nancy and the older girls will bring the ponies back when the show is over. Clearly the right decision, Lynn and Anne are asleep in the car as soon as I back out of our parking space.

Great. With them asleep, I get to play my music on the radio.

Nancy gives all the girls autonomy in many areas, including the music in the pickup. They all have different preferences so music plays in rolling twenty-minute increments.

Nancy likes show tunes, Anne is into rock and heavy metal, and Lynn, and Taylor prefer pop. Dana and I like country western.

I'm not keen about Anne's choice of rock and heavy metal for such a young child, but Nancy disagrees and says Anne has a right to what she likes. I think I heard that Mozart wrote symphonies at the age of three or four. So I guess it's not odd that young children relate to specific music.

It's hard for me to avoid pushing my preferences on the girls. I know Nancy's parents were quite restrictive when she was a child, so I often wonder if she gives our kids the freedom of choice she was denied.

All day I'd forgotten about our precarious financial condition. Now it all comes back in a rush as I think about the choices I want to have available for Lynn's and Anne's future.

48

ZAPPED

There's new money in the bank from the sale of two horses. Also for Widdle, Jane Russell and Rustler, who have moved on to new adoring, and paying, owners. Kurt Russell and Rusty have deposits on them. And Foxy has gone to live with Nancy's friend, as promised.

I earmark most of the money for the mortgage payments. Taking a risk, I spend some on trusses and plywood for the barn roof. The trusses are custom built and really expensive. We need twenty-eight of them.

I'm setting more telephone poles to frame the barn when I happen to glance at the field where Figgy, Whimsey, and several other horses are turned out.

I pause to watch. Figgy and Whimsey graze a few feet from the electric fence.

Figgy moves to place the much smaller Whimsey between him and the fence. With a bump of his hip, he deliberately forces Whimsey against the wire.

When Whimsey hits the electric fence, she jumps in reaction

and runs a few steps away. Figgy puts his head down and continues grazing as if nothing happened.

It was a premeditated action to push Whimsey. I wonder what that was all about?

As I put my tools away for the evening, I find one of Amy's yellow tennis balls in my box. I stare at it for a moment, remembering the pleasurable times shared with Amy at the end of my work day. I shake away the sad feeling and start to replace it in the box when I have a thought. I stuff it in my pocket instead.

After dinner, I sit on the floor in the kitchen, where the puppies are currently confined and roll Amy's ball across the floor. The four puppies are still very young, but their eyes light up. They race, or should I say bounce, after it. The tennis ball is way too big for them to get into their mouths, but they don't care. They play with it by pushing it and herding it around the floor.

The kids gather around to watch. The puppies are having a great time and the kids are having fun cheering them on.

It's nice to see Amy's ball giving pleasure again.

49

MAKING HAY WHILE THE SUN SHINES

I take careful notes as Curtis makes our hay.

Over the course of a couple days, he cuts the hay, laying it flat on the ground in rows to dry. The next day he rakes the rows and turns the hay over so the lower side dries. Then he bales it.

When I ask questions, he tells me never to bale the hay with any moisture.

Bundled tightly in a bale, the moisture causes the hay to mold. The mold is poisonous to horses and if the mold isn't discovered in time, it creates heat. Weeks or months later, the mold can get hot enough to burst into flames.

That's a pretty frightening thought.

I carefully count the number of bales Curtis makes per acre. With about twenty acres available to make hay and approximately fifty bales an acre, that's a thousand bales of hay. At the current rate, that's 2,500 dollars in either savings or sales. Double that for what Curtis says will be a second, but slightly smaller cutting per year. That's a substantial amount.

We could make even more hay if we didn't let the horses use

the eight acres of pasture. But, somehow I don't think I have any chance at convincing Nancy that the horses should be kept in stalls all summer, not that we actually have any stalls yet.

I'm still pleased with the hay deal I made even though we've run into a serious problem. My arrangement with Curtis doesn't include his picking up our portion of the hay and putting it in our shed. I just never thought to ask. I'm so clueless. It doesn't even dawn on me until Curtis and his three friends pick up his half for the larger part of the day.

As I drive in from work, Curtis and his friends wave goodbye on their way out with their last load. Our hay is waiting in the fields.

As they pass, I suddenly realize that he told me that the hay can't sit on the ground overnight or the bottom will absorb moisture. I hurry to the house and warn Nancy. In a panic, Nancy and I hastily throw on barn clothes and race into the field with the pickup truck.

With Nancy driving past the bales, I throw the first few sixty-pound bales into the pickup. Almost immediately a problem with this system appears. Someone needs to be in the pickup to stack the hay as it's tossed in. So I have to climb up into the pickup every time I throw a bale in and stack it. That's taking a huge amount of time per bale and we have limited time to get done before dark.

There's no way this can work.

I have an idea. We obviously need more hands. The twins are here. No, they can't lift bales, but one of them could learn to drive the truck. It only requires leaving the truck in its lowest gear, steering straight, and braking gently. The twins already run the riding lawn mower and the tractor, Dana has even run the backhoe

I hired for work around the farm. They're both used to the concepts of machinery with clutches, gears, and brakes.

Dana volunteers immediately when I ask. Taylor wants to learn too, so I agree to give her a lesson in the next couple days.

A quick learner, Dana grasps what to do in minutes. When we reach the end of the rows, I hop in with her until she's comfortable making the turns. And that's how we work. Dana drives, Nancy stacks, and I throw the bales up into the truck. Then we drive to the shed and unload and stack inside.

It's hard, hot work. By ten o'clock we're forced to stop. We're exhausted and we can feel the night's damp coming on. We manage to save only three hundred of our five hundred bales.

As soon as I'm awake in the morning, I call Curtis. Dialing is not an easy feat since my fingers are swollen and every inch of me is scratched.

"What can we do about the remaining two hundred bales?"

"You could roll them so the bottom's facing the sun as soon as the day warms up and the tops are dry. Best hurry though, my mom says we're going to have a thunderstorm this afternoon."

Off the phone, I quickly check the paper and the morning weather report on TV.

Bright and sunny all week. Not a storm in sight. I breathe a sigh of relief.

We wait until eleven o'clock for the bales to be warm enough and then roll them so the bottoms are on top. Then I take off late for work.

When I get home, we'll pick them up.

I barely manage to crawl into my lab. The hot shower, coffee, and aspirin that I took earlier did nothing to help the utter fatigue I feel. The thought of moving more hay when I get home makes me miserable. I can tell I'm groaning out loud at the thought when some of my coworkers glance at me with concern.

By the time I leave work, my arms are breaking out in an itchy rash from all the hay scratches.

As I cross on the ferry, I notice the sky is dark in the direction of our farm.

No. That can't be right. There's no rain predicted. But there's no mistaking those black clouds. Is it too much to hope that the storm had missed our place?

It is.

As soon as I near home it's clear that the thunderstorm had zeroed in on our area. In Leesburg, everything is dry and promising. As soon as I turn onto 621, the ground is totally soaked.

What is it with Curtis' mom? How can she possibly know the weather better than all the weathermen with their scientific equipment? The woman boggles my mind.

I pause to look at our fields as I pass. Such a waste. The bales are no longer any good for feed. And they have to be removed from the field quickly before they smother the grass they're sitting on. And now, full of water, they'll weigh over a hundred pounds each. Lifting them will be daunting.

When I step in the front door, Nancy and the four girls look at me as if I just landed from a different planet.

Their gasps startle me. Nancy grabs the car keys from me and pushes me back outside.

"We're going to the emergency room," she tells them.

I don't understand.

"Just get in the car. "

I do, but I insist on an explanation.

She starts the motor and back onto the driveway.

"Look in the mirror."

I look and my alarmed gasp matches theirs.

The skin on my face is raw and red.

"What's..., that's poison ivy."

**

In the emergency room, the frowning admittance nurse points me to a distant seat and hands forms to Nancy.

While we wait, my eyes water and I start coughing.

I ask Nancy about her day to keep my mind off my symptoms.

She and the twins noticed the storm coming in and made a grab at getting some of the hay in. They managed another sixty bales between them.

"We didn't stack it in the truck. We'd get some in and then run it to the shed and do it again. What we added to the shed will need to be restacked."

"Every bale helps. We still have to get those bad bales up."

"I called Curtis. He said it would only be good for mulch. He didn't want any. So I called Ken. He's going to call a couple contractors. If they can get it for free, maybe they'll come pick it up. He'll let us know tomorrow."

Even that good news can no longer distract me from the pain I'm in.

I'm relieved when the nurse calls my name. I'm not so relieved with the diagnosis. I have poison ivy, poison oak, and hay fever. The poison ivy and poison oak are bad enough, but having the same allergy as Morris is a low blow. At least nobody tried to give me a drench yet.

**

A couple weeks, a few lost skin layers, and several shots later, I'm out and working again. I'm not sure which was worse. The poisons, the hay fever, or the shots.

I'm needle phobic. In my younger days, I was known to pass out when receiving a shot.

I'm not proud of it, but that's the way my body reacts. Anne is showing signs of needle phobia too. I had no idea it was hereditary.

I enter the shed to restack the last sixty hay bales that Nancy and Taylor saved from the fields. This time I'm dressed better. I have on work gloves, a thick, long sleeved shirt, and a bandana over the bottom half of my face. That should help with the scratchy ends of the timothy and protect me from any poison ivy or oak that got baled with the hay.

There's not much room left in the storage side of the shed. I don't think we could have found room for the bales we lost to the rain. Luckily Ken found a contractor who came for them immediately. It saved us a lot of work.

Nancy's barn equipment is shoved into one corner of the shed. The cat's feed pan sits on top of her show trunk.

When I pick up the first bale, a huge, ginger-colored cat leaps off the top of the stack and dashes out the door.

Wait. We don't have a ginger colored cat. Must be a neighbor's pet.

I pile a few more bales up and pause. My eyes are already starting to swell and I'm sweating. The heat in this closed space is stifling. It was built deliberately with its back to the wind as protection for the horses.

I step outside to get some air. Darn if I don't see another cat. It's got brown and black stripes and is smaller and skinnier than the ginger one. Where are they coming from?

I put the question to Nancy when I get back to the trailer.

"I've seen them too, Nancy says. "I think people are abandoning them along 621. Nan said they've found two new ones up at their place, too."

"You know how I feel about cats. When are they going to the shelter?"

"They're not a problem. There are tons of field mice. When the barn's finished there'll be plenty of room. You'll never see them unless you're in the barn."

"So how many new ones are there?"

"Only five or six."

50

JUNIOR STRIKES OIL (PAINT)

It's another hot summer day in Virginia. Sadly, the ninety percent humidity still bothers a New Englander like me.

When I was stacking hay, I noticed Nancy's painted show equipment trunks and stools were getting dirty and scratched up in the shed. I have a couple hours free, so I decide to pull out all her wooden things and repaint everything. She has a couple of stools, a box with braiding equipment that you can stand on, a small trunk, a portable stand to clean saddles on, plus a few smaller pieces.

I can see Nancy down by the marshy area on the tractor with the bush hog. The area where she's mowing is too marshy to cut hay, as the hay would never dry properly.

It also has a lot of small juniper bushes and saplings from the big oak tree beside the pond. Nancy plans to mow as close as she can to the pond and the run-off area so the trees and bushes don't take over and make the area a jungle. There are already several saplings that are too big to mow, but they'll make nice trees. If only my garden grew as quickly as the brush around the pond.

I hope Curtis doesn't show up. She's in her bathing suit again.

She tells me she enjoys mowing. One of the things she likes best is the barn swallows. They're small dark blue birds with long, forked tail feathers. When the tractor and bush hog chop through the high grass, all sorts of insects leap to get out of the way.

The swallows fly above and beside the slow steady tractor, darting in and out after the insects. The quick maneuvers and graceful dives make for an exciting show.

They're unbelievably fast. I can see them surrounding her from here and I know she's having fun. The swallows turn out for all the haymaking activity, too.

When I first put up the sheds, their mud nests appeared immediately. Over the summer we've watched the nests, then the little chirpy voices, and finally, the babies' heads peeking over the edges.

I look up. The shed's nests are empty today. It's late summer now and all the baby birds have grown and gone. They don't seem to use the nests once the babies learn to fly even though they're still around. I guess they'll head south when the cold weather comes. I'm looking forward to next year's cycle as much as the kids are.

I have to dig to find the can of dark green, outdoor enamel paint that Nancy uses for her equipment. I locate it behind the butter yellow latex paint we just finished painting the sheds with. I'm pleased to find it's almost full. I think of the time Nancy painted the kitchen in Great Falls and chuckle.

Since I know she will park the tractor behind the shed when she's done, I place the equipment out on the field side to paint. The horses are all up in the far corner where there's some shade. The paint will dry quickly in the sun and I can put the things away before the horses come back to the shed.

The work goes quickly. I'm pleased to finish just as she parks the tractor.

I climb under the fence to chat with her.

She's spotted a couple of new woodchuck holes and describes where she saw them.

Woodchucks have the same kind of front teeth as rats and beavers. They live in fairly open fields and dig deep dens with multiple exits. Our hay fields are full of these holes. They're extremely dangerous for horses. Any horse who steps into a woodchuck hole will probably break a leg. Horses rarely survive breaking a leg. They're not good patients and it's difficult for a horse to keep his weight off a leg for the time required to heal it.

When we fenced off the sections for fields, we carefully walked them to be sure there were no such holes. We keep patrolling the turn-out fields to make sure they stay that way.

We do have a secret weapon: Shakey. He single-handedly hunts them. He'll sit quietly for hours, waiting for one to come out. Then he'll grab it and almost immediately dispatch it.

Amazing considering woodchucks have a reputation as fierce fighters and that they weigh around twenty pounds. Shakey never eats them and he never comes to the house with any blood on him. Once he's subdued them, he carries them, no matter how big, down near the pond and buries them where the ground is softer.

He's having a serious and welcome effect on the woodchuck population.

Kablam! A loud noise from where I was painting interrupts our conversation.

What on earth?

I climb back through the fence to check the other side of the shed.

It's Junior.

Of course it is. Who else would it be? Let me rephrase that. Figgy is also a serious possibility.

I never noticed Junior come to the shed.

She's banged into the open can of green enamel and is leaping around, like a whirling dervish, agitated by the thick paint on her tail. She's whipping it furiously. The more upset she's getting, the faster her tail is going.

The butter yellow side of the shed already looks like a Jackson Pollock painting with dark green splashed all over it. The freshly painted barn equipment rolls in the dirt.

Nancy yanks my belt off and grabs Junior around the neck. She pulls her under the open side of the shed.

"Quick, get me a halter. I need to keep her out of the sun."

I grab one from the storage side of the shed and pass it to her. Junior's a little calmer, but her hind feet are still bouncing every time her tail swats her sides.

In minutes, Junior speckles us with green paint as well. I can see why she's upset. When her tail strikes her skin with the paint, it stings like a whip.

"What do we do?" Nancy asks.

"About what?"

"The paint. It's oil based enamel. It only cleans off with turpentine. Turpentine will burn her skin. We have to get it off before it dries."

I freeze. I have no idea what to do.

"Go call the vet. Run."

I race down to the trailer and dial. Thank goodness he's in.

Dr. Clarke grasps the problem immediately.

Cooking oil he says. Any kind, all kinds, Crisco, lard, olive,

274

just be fast. Don't let the paint dry.

I grab two unopened bottles of Crisco oil from the kitchen and dispatch Taylor with it to help Nancy.

Dana, Lynn, Anne, and I search the cabinets for more oil. All we can come up with is half a bottle of olive oil and some canola oil.

I drive those out to the shed.

Yes, the oil seems to be working. Only there's a lot more of Junior than there is oil. Taylor and Nancy are rubbing as hard as they can.

I take off for Ken's and buy every bit of Crisco he has. Gallons, half gallons, quarts -- all of it. He cracks up when he hears why, but helps me get it loaded in the car.

He also warns me there's a robbery ring working in the area. They hit one of the local farm houses.

It doesn't register. I'm too busy thinking about oil and rushing. Ken's still shaking his head and laughing about Junior as I drive off.

With three of us working for another hour, we manage to get most of the enamel off of Junior, including out of her tail. Even in the dark shed, Junior glistens.

I want to make a crack about breading and frying her, but I've learned better.

Even though I'm not serious, there are times when I know Nancy doesn't appreciate my humor.

Having done the best they can, Nancy and Taylor walk Junior down to the trailer where there's a hose to give her a soapy bath to remove what's left.

Thank goodness Buttons was weaned last week and is in the neighbor's barn with Morris and another horse. Otherwise she'd be green too. I can't imagine trying to rub her down with cooking oil.

I glance around. What a mess. Empty plastic bottles, every barn towel we own, pools of half-dry enamel, and all the freshly painted equipment covered with dirt and debris. Yuck. All of it has to be removed before the other horses wander down.

I start by setting the ruined equipment outside the fence where the horses can't reach it. With a shovel, I bury the coagulating paint. I take garbage bags from the car and pick up the ruined towels and trash. I find only one unused quart of Crisco. I can't believe how much oil we went through.

I check for trash in the storage side of the shed before I finish. That's when I hear it. The sound of kittens mewing.

What the...?

CHAPTER 51

IF IT LOOKS LIKE A DUCK

Junior is dry and back out in the field when I tell Nancy, "There are kittens in the shed."

"How many?"

"I didn't look. You don't seem surprised."

"It's not a big deal. Let's go see what we've got." She heads for the shed.

"Where did they come from?"

I'm not pleased with the casual way she's taking this.

"From the usual place, I expect."

Not funny. I give her the dreaded "are you for real" look. Of course she doesn't see it because she's walking away from me. I'd just as soon she didn't see. The look always tends to start an argument.

Inside the shed, she listens a minute, then follows the mews. The kittens are tucked in a pocket of the hay, very close to where I was stacking earlier.

There are two of them, small and sickly looking. Smitty suddenly shows up when Nancy lifts them.

"Uh, oh. Looks like Smitty's the mother," she says.

"I thought she was fixed after Wood and Mary."

"I meant to take her to Dr. Clark's, but I never could catch her when I was going to his office."

"You, of all people, should know better." I shut my mouth. If I'm not careful, I might say something I'll regret. I know it must really have been a slip-up because Nancy is a big advocate for spaying and neutering. Even so, with the vet at our place at least once a week, how could she forget? Every other animal that lives here has been fixed.

Nancy interrupts my thoughts. "These kittens don't look well. They're awfully emaciated and lethargic. Let's take them down to the house. Dr. Clark will be here tomorrow to worm all the animals. He can check them out."

Great. More money for cats we don't even want. Uh, make that, I don't want.

At the trailer, Nancy finds a box and makes a bed in it for the kittens and Smitty.

However Smitty doesn't appear to be too interested in the kittens. She won't stay in the box with them and cries to be let out if we close the bathroom door.

"She's given up on them. Nature's way is to let the ill die."

The girls don't like that.

Dana asks, "Can we feed them?" They brainstorm for a minute and decide to try watered-down chicken broth with an eye dropper. The consensus on milk is that the kittens might not be able to digest cow milk yet.

Dana picks up the white kitten with dark gray spots when she's ready. We all circle around to watch.

That's when I notice, "Look. It doesn't have a tail."

278

Taylor checks the other one. Again no tail.

We all agree that's weird. Maybe something bit their tails? Are they deformed?

Dana holds the eyedropper to the kitten's mouth. She lets a drop fall on its lips.

It licks tentatively. She tries another drop on the lips. The tiny tongue comes out faster.

After a few seconds, Dana places a drop directly in its mouth. It swallows, then mews.

"Try two more drops and then stop. Come back in half an hour and do it again," Nancy suggests.

Next Dana tries the pale gray one. It seems to be barely breathing but takes a little of the mixture.

When we return in half an hour, the pale gray kitten has passed away. The kids wrap the little body in a soft towel, place the towel in a shoe box, and I carry the box outside to bury. I don't like cats, but I feel sad about this one. He's gone before his life has even started.

The next morning, Dr. Clark checks out the surviving kitten. He puts him on a little feeding regimen which happens every few hours. Other than malnutrition, the kitten appears okay.

Lynn asks, "What happened to his tail?"

"He was born without a tail. If Smitty is his mother, than his father was a Manx."

None of us know what that is.

"You've seen pictures of bobcats and lynx?"

We have, but Dr. Clark explains to Lynn and Anne who haven't. He's nice that way. When they get the idea, he goes on.

"A Manx is a type of domestic cat, but they have some physical differences. No tail, obviously, and it's a little hard to see yet, but this little guy has longer back legs than his front legs. Different from your other cats. Manx are really athletic, smart, and great hunters. You might really enjoy this little guy. He's one of the first Manx I've seen in this area."

With all the care from the kids, it isn't long before the Manx kitten is plump and healthy, and almost as wide as he is long. Having no tail really emphasizes his shape.

His long rear legs also make him look like he waddles when he walks.

Lynn wants to name him Quack. Anne want to call him Horton, after the elephant in *Horton Hears a Who*. From the Dr. Seuss book I've been reading her. After some back and forth, they compromise on Duck.

The house gets quieter a few weeks after Duck moves into the trailer. It's late August, and school has begun. We only see the twins on weekends and holidays.

I head to the living room.

Nancy laughs and points behind me.

"Look who's following you."

I turn. There's Duck, about three feet away.

"When does he go out with the other cats?"

"A couple more weeks."

"And Smitty?"

"She's going to Dr. Clark's next week along with all the cats we can round up. He gave us a deal because he knows they were abandoned."

"Good. Otherwise I'll have to get a book and spay her myself."

Nancy gasps. "You wouldn't?"

"No, but I scared you, didn't I?"

She ignores me. "I think that Duck likes you."

"If that's true, then he's not as smart as Dr. Clark said he'd be.

52

DON'T GO INTO THE WOODS TODAY

I'm eating breakfast the next day when I notice Duck sitting right beside my feet. This cat is definitely pushing it. By the time I'm finished, he still hasn't moved.

Without thinking, I give him a tiny piece of bacon. He takes it gently from my finger.

Drat. Why did I do that? Now he'll be a real pest. Thank goodness he goes out with the rest of the cats soon.

It's Saturday. Nancy has an early doctor's appointment with the kids, and the older girls aren't due for another hour, so I offer to do the morning water run to the fields.

On the way to the fields, Shakey does his act with the deer. When he sees them, he barks and runs towards them. The deer go into their part and act frightened, run away and then drop their heads to graze again. It's funny to see the puppies, Snuggles and Tommy, take their cues from Shakey. They too, charge the deer and then rejoin me on the way to the barn when Shakey does. It makes me smile to watch them.

I'm not so pleased to see the barn when I pass it. The trusses for the roof still haven't arrived. The vertical poles are all up as well as the support beams on top of them, but there's nothing more I can do for the moment.

I back the tractor up to the horses' water tubs. The first tub is just inside the fence.

Since Junior and Buttons have moved out of the small field with the second shed while Buttons is being weaned, Nancy's using the small field to alternate turnout time for our horses living in the neighbors' barn. I'll water there next.

I turn off the tractor motor and then walk over to the shed and disconnect the electric fence. I notice Figgy watching me.

"Don't get any ideas, Figgy. In ten minutes it will be on again." I can't believe I said that out loud. I'm talking to a horse. I must really be losing it.

Back at the tub, I clean it out before hooking up the short piece of garden hose to the barrel on the tractor and draining the water into the tub. As I wait for the tub to fill, I glance back at Figgy.

Odd. Figgy has pushed Whimsey against the fence again. The joke's on Figgy this time. The fence is off so little Whimsey won't get shocked.

The thoughts are no sooner in my head than Figgy pushes Whimsey again.

That's simply mean. But with no shock, Whimsey keeps right on grazing.

Wait. What's Figgy doing? Oh, my gosh. He just jumped out. He wasn't trying to be mean to Whimsey, he was using her to test if the electricity was on. Heaven forbid Figgy should test the fence himself. Come to think of it, he is being mean.

I rush into the other side of the shed, grab a halter, dump a handful of grain in a bucket, and race after him.

53

BRAD SAVES THE DAY

Nancy sells Morris. He isn't going to jump well enough to be her next show horse. I can't say I'm sorry he's gone, but she's pretty dejected about it. Going to horse shows gives her a lot of pleasure.

Since she's not showing today, she took all the girls to Warrenton to watch something called a Jack Russell Terrier Trial. According to a brochure she read, there are different classes like a horse show. In one, they're judged on conformation, that's how they're built, like any dog show. The rest of the day consists of dog races and something called "go to ground."

In that last class there's a long artificial tunnel with a rat in a cage at the end.

The Jack Russells are timed from the moment they leave their handler's arms to the moment they reach the end of the tunnel and bark at the rat. Sounds like fun, but I have some work to do on the house trailer.

The morning farm chores are done. The electric fence is on. Figgy and the other horses are quietly grazing.

I wash up from the chores, pour a cup of coffee, and sit down for a ten minute break before I head to the back of the trailer to fix a loose piece of flashing near the roof.

Duck sits beside me as usual. He still follows me around constantly. So much so that earlier this morning Lynn started chanting, "Daddy has a cat. Daddy has a cat."

When I shush her, Nancy stops me.

"She's only telling the truth."

I point behind me at Duck and state very clearly, "That is not my cat."

"Come on. Who sits beside the bed every morning when it's time for you to get up?"

Taylor adds, "I think Duck's the smartest cat in the world. He's figured out who has the say on whether he can stay inside or not."

Everyone nods except me.

I have to agree, he does have unusual behavior. He's allowed out during the day now. Nancy likes him back in at night until he grows big enough to protect himself from raccoons and foxes. We found a den of foxes high on the hill in the middle of the property between the trailer and where the horses are. Interestingly enough, like the deer, the dogs don't seem to bother them.

I thought that trying to find Duck at night to bring him in would be a problem. It hasn't turned out that way.

When the dogs come in with us at dinner time, he's with them.

He'll even go to the door and meow to go in or out when he needs to, like the dogs do. He never uses the kitty litter box we have for him in the house, preferring to go outside instead.

Duck seems to think he's a dog. I don't know if he imprinted

288

on the dogs because there were no other cats in the trailer except Wood occasionally or what. But he has no trouble mixing with the cats when he's out either. With exceptions.

Wood is the alpha male cat. If Wood is near the trailer when it's time for Duck to come inside in the evening, Duck will not be with the dogs. Instead, I'll find him waiting patiently where I park the car when I come home from work.

Knowing Nancy will send me out to find him if he's missing, I scoop him up and carry him into the trailer past Wood. I can almost see him thumb his nose at Wood as he's carried by.

Duck also seems to have a thing for Anne's puppy, Tommy. Tommy's more of a teenaged dog than a puppy now. But Duck will lie in wait, upside down on the trailer stairs for Tommy to have to go in or out. When Tommy tries to pass, Duck will try to scratch his stomach. We try to chase Duck off but it's something he insists on doing. Poor Tommy never seems to get the idea of waiting until someone comes and helps him.

It's funny that Duck doesn't do this with any other dog. Not even the other puppy, Snuggles. At all other times, Duck and Tommy will sleep together in a pile with the other dogs and cats and be perfectly happy together.

Coffee finished, I head out to work on the trailer's flashing. That's the metal sheeting that prevents water from seeping in around the edges of the roofing. I noticed there's a loose area in the back.

**

I'm up on the ladder behind the trailer where I can just see over the edge of the roof. I've cleaned the flashing and given it a coat of sealer on the underside, when a white service van turns into the old farm house in the hollow across from us. That's odd. I know the elderly man who owns it is still in a nursing home. Maybe the driver has the wrong address.

I press down the flashing and begin to screw it in place. That van still hasn't come back to the road. I can't quite see the house clearly through the trees, but there's a bit of white showing that must be the van.

I continue working and then I remember Ken said there were robbers working our area. What if...?

I drop down the ladder and into the back door of the trailer. The dogs follow me in. I grab a pair of binoculars, shut the dogs inside, and return to the top of the ladder. I peek over the trailer roof. I can still see the white of the van between the surrounding trees.

I train the binoculars on the house. The front door is open. I can see feet come out of the house. A minute later they go back in.

I hasten back into the trailer and dial 911. The operator assures me that the sheriff is on his way and tells me to wait inside. I lock up the doors and windows to make it harder for the robbers if they come this way and try to get in.

I'm glad Nancy and the girls are gone. They're not due back for hours. It's only been a couple of minutes but I'm too anxious to stay in the house. I can't see anything from the front windows.

I slip out the back door and climb the ladder cautiously. Using the binoculars, I watch the farm house. The robbers are still there. Gosh, I hope they are robbers. It'd be awful if I called the cops on a neighbor's family members. But I've never seen a car go in or out of that driveway before. Better safe than sorry. At least I know they're not ghosts.

Sirens blaring, two police cars speed in from two different directions and turn in at the farm house. The sheriff and his deputies are quick. As I watch, there's a small scuffle and one of the deputies, after a short foot race, takes down the last man.

With the sheriff and his men in control, I finish screwing down the flashing.

An hour later, there's a knock on the door. It's the sheriff. Beyond him, I see the second police car leave with three men in the back.

"Sheriff Stone. You Brad Smith?"

I nod.

"Same one as with the ghosts, right?"

I nod again, wishing he hadn't remembered.

"I have to admit, we had a few laughs on the way here at your expense. But this time you nailed it. Been trying to catch up with those men for over a year now."

"So they *are* robbers?"

"Very professional gang. Nice to finally have them in lockup."

**

The next time at Ken's store, I'm flabbergasted when I get a round of applause from everyone present, including the Edmonds and Curtis. Apparently Sheriff Stone credited my call with breaking up the ring. Anyone would have done it, but I have to admit, the appreciation feels good.

54

ALL PSYCHED UP

"Take a quick shower. We're due at a party in an hour. A friend wants to introduce me to a lady looking for a horse to buy."

The last place I want to go is a goofy party. I just walked in the door from a trip to London and a week of work with the British Standards Association. There were people there from all the major countries. Computer aided manufacturing and robotics is exploding around the world. It's a very exciting time for my career.

Still, I'm exhausted from the flight home and the mental overload during the trip. I have a big decision to make and then discuss with Nancy. All I want to do is take my shoes off and relax.

But I know that's not fair to her. She's been carrying the responsibility for the family for a week. My work friends tell me their wives complain whenever they travel for work. There's no extra pay for the time spent away from home or even the travel time. Nancy never complains and I do travel a lot. She deserves a night out.

We're on our way before I think to ask, "So what kind of party is it this time?"

"I think it's drinks and dessert. No theme." That's a relief.

There turn out to be about sixteen people. The desserts are great, giving me a little sugar boost. I find a glass of merlot, and I do relax a bit. I can see Nancy on the far side of the room chatting with her friend and the prospective buyer.

The house is decorated with the standard for Leesburg and Middleburg-horse paintings and antique furniture. The well worn upholstered furniture is deep and comfortable.

When I sit, I can barely manage to keep myself from nodding off to sleep so I force myself to get up and mingle. I only really know one or two people there, and I mostly nod my head and listen to the gossip flowing around me.

"Her husband caught them in bed and shot him dead."

"Did he shoot her, too?"

"She crashed through the plate glass window naked and managed to run to a neighbor's house."

"That expensive new horse Evelyn bought is lame. She's suing the sellers."

"-- so he came home drunk to find she'd changed all the locks on the doors."

"I heard he stood in the front yard and yelled. Then his wife opened the window and threw all his clothes into the yard."

"A neighbor called the police."

"There wasn't anything he could do. The house is in her name and she told Sheriff Stone and her husband to get off her property."

Our area gossip is wilder than the latest soap opera.

I'm thinking about how I can get Nancy to leave early when a hush falls over the room. Our host passes out a pen and some papers to each person. It appears there is a theme tonight. We're all taking, for the fun of it, the Meyers Briggs Personality test.

Oh, great. Another psychology test.

I lock eyes with Nancy across the room. She knows my opinion of this kind of stuff. She shrugs.

All around me people seem excited. I join Nancy and hope we can leave before taking the test.

Not a chance. She can't wait to do it. I surrender and start marking the multiple choice questions. I have a fleeting thought. I wonder what the outcome will be if I don't bother to read the questions and just randomly pick the answers. Could be fun.

On second thought, that might not be so smart if the result says I'm a serial killer. Nancy's friends might not believe me if I point out I didn't really take the test. I better read the questions and answer properly.

Do they have psych tests for animals? Be interesting to see what Meyers Briggs can make of Figgy and Junior.

Half an hour later, I sincerely wish we'd gone home earlier. While some of the test is interesting and I have to admit, fairly on the nose, there's one section that, like the *Cosmopolitan* magazine test Nancy took back in Great Falls, doesn't speak well for our marriage.

When our personality type results are compared in the relationship section of the Meyers Briggs manual, it says there is no data available on relationships between our two types because they couldn't find any examples of it when creating the test. That being the case, they didn't feel a relationship between two people of our personality types would work.

What do they know? It's just a stupid test. Nancy laughs it off, but for some reason it gets under my skin.

I'm ready to leave. Since she's met with the possible buyer, we do.

I have news to break to Nancy, but I decide to wait until tomorrow.

55

GO WEST, YOUNG MAN

Today may be a life changer for me, but I can't avoid it any longer. Was the Meyers Briggs test we took last night an omen?

Breaking my news to Nancy will be the hardest thing I've ever done. I have no idea how she'll take it. Will she hate me? Leave me? I can't bear the thought.

But it has to be done. I'm the one responsible for the financial health of our family. I've had to make a hard decision.

I can't get Nancy alone until after dinner. With the kids finally asleep, we sit down in the living room. I keep the TV off and plunge in.

"Honey, we have to talk." My solemn expression immediately alarms her.

I continue, "Our finances are in serious trouble. We have to make some changes."

She doesn't respond. I can see the panic in her face.

"There's no way we can continue paying for both properties. It just can't go on."

"I know."

"There are the kids to think of. We need to start saving for their school.

She nods slowly.

"The horses are not carrying their weight."

"That's because we had to pare them down with no barn. As soon as it's finished I can --"

"In London, there was a man from the Air Force. He offered me a job in California. I'd be working with satellites and launch programs. It's almost double my current salary. I think we should take it."

"We'd have to sell both properties?"

"Yes."

"Can we buy a farm in California?"

"We'll have to check, but I doubt it. The job is in Los Angeles. I hear the land's really expensive in that area." I can see she's stunned.

"People with my experience are at a premium right now. It's the perfect time to switch jobs. I'm sorry honey, but we need to do this."

Her silence is unnerving me. I go to put my arm around her. She waves me off and leaves the room.

I don't know what to do.

I can hear the water running in the bathtub and catch a whiff of the pine-scented bubble bath. She won't be out for hours.

**

I'm waiting miserably in the living room when she finally emerges.

The kitchen clock strikes midnight, before she comes in wearing her robe and smelling faintly of pine. I open my arms and she curls up in my lap.

298

"Why didn't you tell me last night?"

"I was afraid of the answer. I still am."

She doesn't understand.

"Whether you'll choose me or the horses."

"If I have to choose..."

She gives me a long, soft kiss.

Thank goodness.

"I'm sorry it's ending this way," I say.

"How soon do we have to go?"

"I have to be there next month. But you and the girls can come later. I'll come back to help close up things."

"And all the animals?"

Surprised by how reasonably she's taking it, I try to be generous.

"I guess we could take some of the cats and dogs."

She shakes her head.

"Wood and Smitty won't be happy in the city. Shakey won't like it either, but he's getting older. I think he'll be okay."

"So the three dogs and Duck?"

"Maybe we can find a riding place for the kids in Los Angeles. I know they'll miss the ponies terribly."

It's a given she will, too.

Like when the log cabin farm was sold by mistake, I can tell she's trying to adjust to what she considers a devastating situation and move forward.

She gets up and heads for the bedroom.

My heart feels her agony. I truly hate being the cause of pain. I have doubts too, but my logic insists it's the right thing to do.

**

The next afternoon, Vance arrives. Nancy spots his car from

299

the kitchen window. He doesn't come to the door, which may be a smart move on his part.

He pulls a for sale sign from the car's trunk and proceeds to hammer it into the ground in front of the trailer.

As Nancy watches him, I can see her flinch with each blow Vance strikes.

56

IT'S AN ILL WIND

How fitting. Only two weeks until I leave for California and we're going to be hit with another hurricane.

Correction. Another serious hurricane. Every couple of years, there's been one that has manages to reach us, but, unlike Agnes, they're usually just rainstorms by the time they get here.

The coming hurricane is one of the bad ones.

Fluctuating between a tropical storm and a hurricane, Eloise has hit the west coast of Florida with 125 mile-an-hour winds. As it travels north, some newscasters are comparing Eloise to Agnes because of the floods created by its torrential rains. Deaths have already been reported in the Caribbean and Florida.

The high winds worry me most. By the time Agnes reached us, the winds were low for a hurricane, but they were never as high as Eloise's to start with.

The timing couldn't possibly be worse.

The new trusses for the barn roof arrived two weeks late. I had already set all the vertical telephone poles and the double two-by-twelve horizontal support beams.

With Jim's help, I finally got the last of the trusses up yesterday. The whole 110-foot length of trusses is only cross braced by a few two-by-fours, making them highly vulnerable to wind damage.

Eloise is predicted to arrive around ten tonight. I can only hope the temporary cross bracing is sufficient to support the trusses in the high winds they're forecasting. The wind is expected to drop to ninety miles an hour, but that's still much higher than Agnes.

Paying for the trusses, the plywood, which hasn't been delivered yet, and the roofing out of a couple horse sales and the puppy sales was a huge risk. I know the property will sell better if the barn is enclosed. If the trusses are destroyed in the storm...well, I don't even want to think about that.

The basic reality is that we need more money. The better paying job in California is important. Our two growing kids take priority. I know Nancy's upset about the move, but she'll get over it. I hope.

I try to ignore all the deep sighs and wounded looks, but I'm only human. They hurt.

In the meantime, I need to get both these properties sold.

I follow the hurricane news carefully over the day. There's no reduction in the wind predictions by evening. This afternoon, Nancy and I moved all the horses into the neighbors' barn.

Still, I'm getting more and more nervous. House trailers like the one we live in are notoriously dangerous in any major wind events. There's no way for me to predict how the hurricane will affect it. We have it tied down with augers into the ground and straps, but that is only good for normal situations. Sitting up on cinder blocks, the wind has access to all six sides of the trailer.

The rain starts around dinner time. The wind rises around eight o'clock. So does my anxiety level.

I decide to be safe rather than sorry.

I wake up Lynn and Anne. Nancy catches my worry and we're in total agreement. We carry the sleepy kids and place them in blankets in the back of the car with Shakey, Snuggles, and Tommy. Smitty, Wood, Mary, and Duck follow in two cat carriers. Nancy adds some flashlights, snacks, and water. She stays with them while I try to secure the trailer by turning off anything connected to power and disconnecting the propane for the stove.

When I finish, I drive the car with my family behind the trailer and park it about twenty-five feet behind it, facing into the wind. The major gusts seem to be coming from that direction. I'm hoping the car will act as a bit of a wind break for the trailer. If the trailer does go, it will go away from the car. The car should still be in a safe position. After that, we hunker down to wait out the storm.

With all the bodies packed in a small space, there's no need for the heater. Lynn and Anne fall back to sleep immediately. Even the pets settle in. Nancy dozes on and off.

Not me.

Between the dark and the rain it's impossible to see anything. With the family secure, I can't stop worrying about the possible loss of the expensive trusses and the hit to our finances. Every time the car sways in a gust, I imagine the trusses swaying.

Finally, I can't sit still anymore.

"I'm going back to check the barn." I stuff a flashlight into my pocket.

"There's nothing you can do. Stay here."

"I have to know. I won't be long."

303

"Promise me you won't do anything risky."

"If I blow away, look for me in the next state."

"Not funny."

I struggle to force the car door open and manage to get out during a lull between gusts.

The wind almost knocks me over and I'm soaked instantly. Maybe I should get back in the car. No, I have to see. No point in stopping now.

I manage to hike back to the barn.

Braced against one of the vertical telephone poles, I aim my flashlight upward.

The trusses are all up, but they're bending and flexing in the wind. They could come down at any minute.

Without thinking, I grab a hank of rope from among my stashed barn building supplies. Jim and I had been using the rope to raise the trusses. Finding my ladder, I tie it to a vertical support with baling string and climb.

The wind rips at me and it's all I can do to hang on. I try to add support for the trusses by weaving the rope in and out, but everything is wet and slippery. The footing is treacherous. When I almost plunge off the roof, I finally realize that what I'm doing is extremely dangerous.

I give it up. I'm trudging miserably back toward the car when, out of the nowhere, comes a shocking realization.

I don't want to leave the farm. I achingly, heartbreakingly don't want to go.

Of course, I love my family. Yet somehow, in spite of all the problems, I've come to love our life on the farm. There's serenity to living here, a feeling that I'm part of the universe. I truly enjoy the personal satisfaction of building things with my own two hands.

The antics of the animals amuse me. I get up in the morning smiling, and looking forward to each day. How many people are that lucky?

Do I really want to give that up for more money?

When I get back to the car, I'm too shocked by my thoughts to share them with Nancy. For the next few hours, as the car rocks in the wind and my family sleeps around me, I try to make a decision. Go for the money we desperately need with the new job or stay in debt in the life I've come to unknowingly love?

Around midnight, the wind and rain drop in intensity. I wake Nancy and we move everyone back into the trailer. Checking the radio, I confirm that the worst is over.

Still, sleep doesn't come. It's a long night.

First one up, I make the morning coffee. I can see the neighbor's barn with our horses from the window and everything looks fine. I feed the dogs, then fill Duck's small dish with his chicken broth and kibbles. He keeps me company as I start breakfast.

I should go out and check the trusses, but I realize I'm putting off the agony of seeing them all busted up.

The kids love pancakes. I still believe that after such an upsetting night a treat is in order. A little comfort food will be good for Nancy and me too, before we deal with all the day's problems.

I glance outside as I stir the batter. There are trees with branches down and everything is drenched. But there, in the middle of the front yard, and totally unaffected by the storm, is the for sale sign. My eyes fixate on it. Seconds later, I find myself standing over it and it's flat on the ground. I have no memory of knocking it down.

When I look up, Nancy stands in the trailer doorway, concern written on her face.

I smile at her.

"We're staying."

57

THE MORNING AFTER

As I expected, my first view of the barn is gut wrenching. Not a single truss stands.

They litter the ground like toothpicks, twisted, bent, and broken. Of course our insurance won't cover a partially built barn.

I'm devastated, but oddly not as deeply as I would have been last night.

I inspect the mess carefully. The vertical telephone poles and the two-by-twelve cross beams haven't budged an inch. The sheds are intact with the exception of the loss of some roll roofing. That's an easy repair. I even have some material left over. That's the good news.

Then there are the trusses. A few of the trusses managed to fall intact. Some I might be able to repair, others I know I can't.

Nancy joins me for a look. The hug we share means more than words.

I hook the chain for pulling things out of the mud to the tractor and drag the trusses apart, spreading them out individually. Each one is thirty-two feet wide by twelve feet high in a triangular shape. Once I do that, I can inspect them closer and get a better idea of what can be saved. I find myself whistling as I work. My realization last night has lifted a great load off of my chest.

Nancy walks the field fences to check for holes and problems. She carries a bag of haywire saved from bales of hay and a roll of duct tape.

Haywire is one of the most important pieces of equipment on a farm. We constantly use it as a repair or a stop gap repair. It's the first thing we grab when something needs to be fixed. On the farm, things need to be repaired constantly.

Especially with Figgy living here.

The second item in her bag is duct tape. Whoever invented duct tape should be put on a pedestal and praised. No tool kit should ever be without haywire and duct tape.

The horses all weathered the storm well at the neighbors'. Nancy will bring them home as soon as we're sure their fields and sheds are safe.

We made some calls earlier. Jim and Nan survived the hurricane safely also.

Nancy's parents arrive after we eat and watch Lynn and Anne while we work.

Inspecting the trusses takes me most of the day. Out of the twenty-eight trusses we bought, nine are intact. I think I can mend thirteen. The other six are rubbish.

As I work, an idea pops into my head.

The vertical telephone poles and cross beams are set for a one-hundred and ten foot barn. But what if we shortened the barn to eighty-two feet? With twenty-two trusses, I'll have enough to cover that. Will thirty feet less make that much difference?

Later, as I help Nancy load Junior and Buttons to come

home, I raise the subject.

She easily agrees to the change in barn length. I think she's so happy we're staying, she'd agree to anything today. That's a situation I should take advantage of, but who could ask for more than I already have?

58

IF YOU CAN'T BEAT 'EM

A Year Later

Our log cabin farm finally sold a month after Hurricane Eloise. That lifted the huge financial burden from us.

Standing in the window of our new prefab house with Duck in my arms, I can see Anne, barely taller than the hay at some points, hiking across the fields. She's leading the pony, Whimsey, and followed by Shakey, Tommy, Snuggles, and Wood fanned out behind her. Our newest rescue dog, Christy, races to catch up.

Christy's a wonderful dog. The pound alerted us about her. I'm sure we're on their speed dial. She's very smart and fits right in with the rest of our animals. She's a Vizsla, slightly smaller than Shakey, maybe forty-five pounds, and a nice chestnut color with a pink nose. Interestingly, Shakey seems to have taught her to smile, too. It's fun when both of them smile at you at the same time.

Anne's chosen a lovely fall day for a picnic.

She'll find a nice spot and have the lunch she carries in a paper bag. It's packed with pet treats too. She usually picks a spot with grass for the pony and the other animals will search the surrounding area and bask in the sun until it's time to return.

It's one of her favorite things to do. From the look of the animals, they enjoy it too.

Anne currently co-holds the local fishing title for the biggest carp. She and a neighbor's boy were fishing in nearby pond. When the boy hooked a carp, he couldn't successfully drag it to solid ground where he could control it. When it got close to the edge, Anne waded in and sat on it. Between the two of them, they managed to get the fish onto land. The boy's father drove them down to Ken's to weigh it officially and it was a new record.

Watching Anne and the animals, I have to think farm kids lead a very different life than city kids. I help myself to a croissant and get a kitty treat for Duck.

Before I leave the kitchen, I make an addition to the grocery list. Buy calamine lotion. I felt a couple scratchy spots this morning. Then Duck and I sit out on the front porch to enjoy the day, and so I can keep an eye on Anne's picnic.

I can see Nancy and Lynn down at the barn washing Lynn's pony for a show tomorrow. Lynn loves competing with her pony. She's written a paper for school about what she learned from riding in shows. It was surprisingly mature and she made some interesting points. Time management is one thing she listed. Being at the show ring gate, properly dressed, pony groomed, and warmed up, ready for their turn in the ring.

Nancy lets the kids have any pets they want, even the snakes and bugs that Anne likes to bring home, although the rule for wild animals is that they have to live in the garage and must be released in two days. The only other rule is that the kids have to take care of them. That includes feeding and grooming in the afternoons and picking ticks off the dogs and cats in the summer.

Lynn also mentions in her school paper that prizes are not always a reflection of accomplishment. Fifth place in a horse show class with excellent competition might mean a great ride on her part, whereas a first in another class might reflect a lower level of personal achievement. She's learned to judge her performances on whether she's improving, rather than the prizes she wins. Her paper impressed me. I had never thought of riding in those terms. Of course, this is the same Lynn who was asked to write about something green in the refrigerator and chose the moldy cheese on the bottom shelf.

Nancy still doesn't "do domestic." I can see my new garden from here, too. I finally found a way to garden that works for me. It's called square-foot gardening. I don't know who came up with the idea, but it's a great one.

Nancy saw something about it on TV and told me. It doesn't work for corn which needs long rows, but I don't grow that any more. I laid out a grid of old railroad ties to create one-foot squares between them. Then I filled those squares with a specially prepared mix of compost and top soil to form raised planters. Next, I separate my baby plants when they're large enough and place an appropriate number in each square. The plants are easy to weed and water, and they seem to be thriving. Not exactly the two-acre garden I started with at the log cabin farm, but finally I have a manageable garden that yields food.

Off to the side of my garden is a space we're preparing for an afternoon Combat Croquet party and picnic next week. It's something Nancy dreamed up out of an old croquet set we inherited from her family. The game will be a combination of croquet, miniature golf, and our favorite: water fights.

313

Participants are going to use wooden croquet mallets and balls to complete a laid out course in the backyard. For example, one wicket involves a ramp that rolls the ball up to a hole between stacked hay bales. If you don't hit the ball hard enough, and we secretly rigged it so you can't, the ball will fall on the far side of the hay into the kids' old wading pool filled with water. If that happens, that player will have to draw a poem from a bowl and recite it while standing in the pool.

"I'm a Little Teapot" is an example of the level of poetry choices.

Guests are invited to come armed with water pistols. I figure if I can't avoid our horsey friends' love of weird parties, I might as well join them.

Things have changed a bit since our first years of marriage. I hated all of the psychological tests Nancy used to read that said our marriage wouldn't survive. Thank goodness we never listened to them. Although I do admit there were times they made me pretty darn nervous.

I stifle a chuckle remembering all the long-gone, child-raising books I read. I was so worried about having children.

A co-worker named Fred recently approached me. I admit I'm a bit of a joke at work. When the gang heads out for happy hour at the local bar after work in Gaithersburg, I'm often rushing home, hoping I can catch enough daylight to bale hay.

As the butt of many office jokes, I'm surprised when Fred asks if he can talk about something personal.

"I admire how well behaved your kids were at the company picnic last week and how cool you are with them. I didn't dare bring my boys. They're so hyper and never listen to anything I say. They're driving me crazy. What's your secret?"

At that moment, I realized I'd become a different father than I'd ever expected. Having the twins, Izzy, and all our wonderful animals around, has totally relaxed my perspective on life. I especially remember the day that I understood that I should be a teacher, not a dictator.

I also like that there's never a shortage of cross-generation conversation on the farm. As for me, I've learned to treat all the girls as individuals, regardless of age. As Nancy always says, they're young, not stupid. And it's true.

We've all learned so much from the animals. The cats and dogs give unconditional love. The horses teach motor skills and partnership. All the animals teach responsibility, confidence, and problem solving. Because of them, everyone at the farm is busy and happy in their own individual way. Myself included.

My advice for Fred?

"Get them each a puppy or a kitten."

EPILOGUE

Brad, Nancy, and their daughters went on to form Equine Resources, a successful horse show management firm. They ran horse shows to raise money for Frying Pan Park in Herndon, Virginia, a Fairfax County facility. They also managed the Whimsey Hill Farm Schooling and Rated shows, the Middleburg National Horse Show, and created the Middleburg-Lexington National Horse Show, now called the Lexington National Horse Show.

**

Brad built their dream house on the hill in the back of the farm as planned. It was the same hill where the deer grazed. The deer continued to graze there even after the house was built, visiting regularly in the fall after Nancy planted two apple trees in the yard. Nancy and Brad lived there until they retired.

**

As of 2012, the beautiful oak trees were still safe on the log cabin property. The log cabin and the big red barn were the same under the care of its current owners. The Smith's second farm on Route 621 continues to exist as a horse farm, even though suburbia is knocking at the gate.

**

Nancy passed Figgy on to another family in nearby Leesburg with appropriately aged kids when Lynn and Anne graduated to horses. On the first day, Figgy locked his new owners in their tack room. Another day, when they closed him in his stall before a show, he promptly walked through the wall to get out. Rumor has it that he had passed away at a ripe old age in the Roanoke, Virginia area, much beloved by riding students at a local riding center.

**

Junior passed away when she at age twenty-five. Somewhere a huge mud puddle in the sky awaited her .

**

The two willow trees Nancy planted in the mud holes were nearly forty feet tall and roughly six feet around when Brad and Nancy left the farm. They did indeed dry the spots out. Snuggles, Christy, and Shakey, as well as many other wonderful small animals are buried under one of them. Every summer the kids hung pots of flowers in its branches in remembrance of the special animals there. Interestingly, the living cats and dogs would frequently lie together in the shade of that specific willow tree, but they never dug there.

**

A few months after Morris (Sailor's Legend) was sold, Nancy acquired another rescue racehorse. It was a mare, also by the local stallion, Sailor. She too liked to step on feet. The twins promptly nicknamed her Mora, short for Mora the Same. A word of warning: watch your feet anytime you're near a Sailor offspring.

**

Nancy and Brad never saw or met Curtis' mom. Nor did anyone we knew except Ken.

Perhaps she was like the mother in Hitchcock's movie *Psycho*. Mummified and sitting in a rocking chair.

**

Sharon lives in northern California after a career as a technical artist with the Navy. She shares her home with several border collies and a corgi. She also teaches obedience classes for dogs and their owners.

**

With the eventual encroachment of the suburbs to Route 621, Jim and Nan moved to a farm further out in rural Virginia where they raise cattle and trail ride in the mountains.

**

Taylor lives on a farm in Berryville, Virginia with her husband, two daughters and nine horses. Dana moved to Florida where she does a lot of volunteer work with animals and children, as well as marine life.

**

Anne still rides occasionally on vacations. She lives in Los Angeles and is very into the rock and heavy metal music scene. Tommy was her constant companion until he passed away at age twenty-four.

**

After a career in entertainment public relations in Los Angeles, Lynn now lives in the Richmond/Charlottesville, Virginia area with three rescue dogs, two rescue cats and six chickens. She enjoys organic gardening, cooking, writes for local newspapers, and is the winner of their local chili competition. She volunteers

319

for riding programs for children with special needs.

**

Brad led and helped create the development and implementation of two major industry projects, IGES (Initial Graphics Exchange Specification), the American National Standard and STEP (Standard for the Exchange of Product Model Data), the International Standard, while at the National Institute of Standards & Technology during the period of this book. These projects are tools still in use by industry today in day-to-day production worldwide.

**

Brad and Nancy have been married forty-seven years as of the writing of this book. Good thing they never listened to *Cosmopolitan* or Meyers Briggs.

If you enjoyed "The Reluctant Farmer,"
please consider leaving a few words of review at
http://Amazon.com

To all of the wonderful young people
who spent time at Whimsey Hill,
Nancy and Brad would love to hear from you.

Please support your local animal shelter

If you would like to find out more about
Whimsey Hill Farm, go to
http://TheReluctantFarmerOfWhimseyHill.com

OTHER BOOKS BY THE AUTHORS

BENCH TIPS FOR JEWELRY MAKING

by Bradford M. Smith

"Bench Tips for Jewelry Making" contains 101 of the most popular and useful bench tips organized into ten main problem areas designed to help you to work efficiently and get quality results. The book is filled with close-up photos and has a detailed index to help quickly find the solution you need.

"Bench Tips for Jewelry Making" contains 101 useful bench tips to help improve skills and increase quality at the bench. It includes 96 pages and is filled with close-up photos to explain the techniques. It is a valuable bench guide and makes a great gift for a friend who makes jewelry.

"Bench Tips for Jewelry Making" is written as a resource for jewelers with skill levels from beginner through advanced. The bench tips come from Brad Smith's 17 years of experience in the jewelry industry, including a decade teaching hundreds of students. They include over 20 ways to save time when soldering and polishing, 8 common hazards to avoid, many ways to cut costs, and 10 tips to improve stone setting skills.

Available   on   Amazon   http://amzn.to/1Z6hQ06

BROOM CASTING FOR CREATIVE JEWELRY

by Bradford M. Smith

Discover the rush of pouring molten silver into a common broom to get marvelous icicle-like shapes that just beg to be designed into finished jewelry such as elegant pendants and earrings.

"Broom Casting for Creative Jewelry" gives step-by-step procedures for casting and covers proper use of all equipment. It includes chapters on how to work with the irregular shapes for your designs and has suggestions for safety, tips for cleaning & polishing, and even ideas for saving money by making some of your own tools.

Written for beginner to advanced jewelers, the book also contains a gallery of finished jewelry incorporating broom cast pieces and a detailed list of equipment needed to run your own workshop for friends or members of your local gem and mineral club.

Available on Amazon   http://amzn.to/1Z6hYws

SUMMERCHASE

by Lynn Raven

Available 2017

LAND SHARKS - A SWINDLE IN SUMATRA

by Nancy Raven Smith

A fall from grace costs Lexi Winslow a position at a top New York financial institution. She ends up in a job at a small private bank in Beverly Hills. But that's okay, she still gets to work in her favorite field - catching white collar crooks. At least that's what she tells herself.

But when Karista, the daughter of one of the bank's principal investors, runs into danger while traveling in Indonesia, Lexi's job comes to depend on her ability to save her. Even worse, Lexi will have to baby sit Steve, her boss' well-meaning but spoiled son, while going undercover to reach the heiress.

Lexi's cushy tropical assignment soon spirals into chaos as she has to outrun fashion-forward Batak natives, outwit an arrogant FBI agent, help Steve find his stolen Air Yeezy sneakers, and figure out why her ardent former lover and debonair gentleman thief, Andre, is staying at the same resort. Lexi will have to be very good or very lucky to survive it all.

Available on Amazon   http://amzn.to/1JuIHku

.

ABOUT THE AUTHORS

BRADFORD M. SMITH

Smith's early professional career with the U.S. Navy and the Department of Commerce in Washington, D.C. focused on manufacturing technology and computer-aided design. The resulting technologies developed by Smith are now widely used in the aircraft and automotive industries worldwide. He helped write numerous industry and government publications, and has presented speeches all over the world. As an adult school teacher, he has self published two how-to books to support his students.

While his work environment was highly technical, his home life was not. With his family, he built and managed Whimsey Hill Farm. Smith partnered with his wife in a horse show business which included annual sporting events with over 1000 equine competitors. The couple was frequently featured in equestrian-related magazines, newspapers, and local publications. Smith says that the contrast between the farm and technology gave him the best of both worlds.

LYNN RAVEN

Lynn Raven was born and raised in the horse country of Northern Virginia. For nearly twenty years, Raven was an award-winning entertainment publicist on both coasts including at The Paley Center for Media (as Associate Director, Public Relations) and National Geographic Society. Always writing stories, Raven attended creative writing classes at University of California, Los Angeles, and has written several feature film screenplays. She was a finalist for the Diane Thomas Screenwriting Award at UCLA and the Houston International Film Festival. She also took media writing classes at UCLA, Georgetown University, and George Washington University in Washington, D.C.

Retired from show biz, Raven lives in Virginia on Whimsey Hill 2 where she continues to write as well as works for a local non-profit. She is a member of Romance Writers of America, Virginia Romance Writers, James River Writers, and Sisters in Crime.

NANCY RAVEN SMITH

Nancy Raven Smith grew up in the Virginia horse country near Washington D.C. where she was an active member of the equestrian community. Not only did she compete on the national level, but Raven Smith also rescued and retrained former racehorses for over 20 years. Raven Smith was a contributing writer and cartoonist to several sports magazines including The Chronicle of the Horse and Practical Horseman.

After relocation to Los Angeles, she worked primarily as a production coordinator on films, music videos, and theater projects. To broaden her skills, she enrolled at the University of California, Los Angeles to study screenwriting and nonfiction writing. SCRIPT magazine chose Raven Smith for its "Hot Sheet" column featuring accomplished, up-and-coming screenwriters.

Her feature film screenplays have won awards and recognition from competitions such as Slamdance Film Festival and the Disney Fellowship. Several of her scripts have been optioned. Raven Smith's debut mystery novel, Land Sharks – A Swindle in Sumatra was chosen as an Amazon/Kindle Scout Program Selection Winner.

She is a member of Women in Film, Sisters in Crime, Mystery Writers of America, and Romance Writers of America.

Author's Note

This work is a memoir. For storytelling purposes and pace, some aspects of the time line have been compressed. In addition, some names and identifying characteristics of people have been altered or combined out of respect for their privacy.

Printed in Great Britain
by Amazon